W9-ANI-577

The Future of the United Nations

Raymond Carroll

Franklin Watts An Impact Book
New York/London/Toronto/Sydney/1985

Photographs courtesy of:
the United Nations: pp. 9, 33, 58, 71, 76, 88, 96;
AP/Wide World: p. 20.

Library of Congress Cataloging in Publication Data

Carroll, Raymond.
The future of the United Nations.

(An Impact book)
Bibliography: p.
Includes index.
Summary: Examines the history, development, and
accomplishments of the United Nations and addresses
the problems and the future of the organization.
1. United Nations—Juvenile literature.
[1. United Nations]   I. Title.
JX1977.Z8C37 1985   341.23   85-7533
ISBN 0-531-10062-6

CONTENTS

THE FUTURE OF
THE UNITED NATIONS

The United Nations reflects both aspiration and a falling short of aspiration, but the constant struggle to close the gap between aspiration and performance now, as always, makes the difference between civilization and chaos.

Dag Hammarskjold

INTRODUCTION

As it begins its fifth decade, the United Nations—once widely regarded as mankind's best hope for survival in a dangerous world—has come under intense and disturbing fire. Of course the world body has been subject to criticism since its inception in 1945, but today the attacks on the organization are more disconcerting in that the sharpest jabs are coming from the United States, once the chief proponent of the United Nations and still its chief financial supporter.

AN IMPERFECT INSTRUMENT

It was understood from the start that the United Nations was an imperfect instrument. As many commentators have pointed out, the very name "United Nations" is a misnomer, a judgment difficult to quarrel with. At a glance, one sees little that unites the 159 countries comprising the membership of the organization in the mid-1980s. They are divided and subdivided along lines of geography, history, ethnicity, religion, language, ideological tenets and goals, national ambitions, and degrees of poverty or prosperity. This state of affairs is unlikely to change significantly in our lifetime.

Still, this divided family of nations does have some profoundly important things in common. To state the obvious, they inhabit the same planet. They share a common humanity. With a few irresponsible exceptions, these sovereign states are united in hoping to preserve the earth's bounty and improve the lives of their people. In varying degrees, they recognize that technological advances have led to an increasing interdependence among the economies of nations. Most important, they are united in their fear of a nuclear war that would plunge the world into an indescribable holocaust and a new Dark Age. In short, these nations, from the puniest of mini-states to the nuclear-armed superpowers, occupy one world. It is the business of the United Nations to help them live together in it.

It is no easy task. The United Nations is in no sense a "world government." The only power it wields is the power bequeathed by its members. French President Charles de Gaulle used to refer to the United Nations somewhat scornfully as *ce machin* ("the machine"), and in fact that is what it is: a complex piece of diplomatic machinery. It is there to be used, disused, or abused, as its members see fit. There is little sense in lambasting the United Nations. If it often seems to function inadequately, that is almost always the fault of its members, not of the organization itself.

MEMBER STATES AND CIVIL SERVANTS

The membership of the United Nations mirrors the political realities of the times. When the organization was created in 1945, its fifty-one charter members came largely from North and South America, Western Europe, and the Soviet bloc of Eastern European states. Since then, the membership has changed radically. As former colonies gained independence in the decades that followed, they eagerly joined an organization in which their sovereignty was respected and their voices heeded. Whereas the West, particularly the United States, dominated the United Nations in its early years, today the so-called Third World countries in Africa, Asia, Latin America, the Caribbean, the Pacific region, and elsewhere are numerically superior. Of course these countries are not always of one mind, but when their interests coincide, as they do on many economic and social issues, they speak with a collective voice that dominates debate and produces hefty voting majorities.

Some observers have said that the United Nations is nothing more than the aggregate of governments represented in it at any given time. There may be some truth in this view, but it neglects the very important role of the United Nations Secretariat. Currently headed by Javier Perez de Cuellar of Peru, this is the permanent structure, the administrative machinery of the organization. It is comparable to the civil service in many countries. Governments come and go; the Secretariat remains. Its more than 25,000 staff members, who work at UN headquarters in New York City and in offices around the world, administer peacekeeping operations, organize conferences, study economic and social trends, prepare studies on disarmament and human rights, and provide translation and interpreting services for member states. The Secretariat is not a policy-making body, but its members cannot help but influence programs—established by the Security Council, the General Assembly, or other UN organs—as they administer them day-to-day.

AMERICAN DISENCHANTMENT

So, when we talk about the United Nations we are talking about (1) the member states and their governments as they conduct themselves in the various bodies in the organization, and (2) the Secretariat itself. Both have come under severe criticism in Western Europe, and particularly, in the United States. In 1983, for example, the U.S. State Department publicly deplored the "politicization" of the United Nations Educational, Scientific and Cultural Organization (UNESCO). It attacked its appallingly bad administrative practices and informed the UN that the United States would drop its membership in UNESCO in 1985 unless drastic reforms were made. (The U.S. formally withdrew at the end of 1984.)

Political leaders on both sides of the aisle in Congress applauded the move, while writers in publications of diverse political persuasions pondered the value of United States membership in the United Nations. Some analysts wondered whether the United Nations could last much longer without a serious overhauling. Opinion polls showed that the American people, though still in favor of membership in the United Nations, had become intensely skeptical about its effectiveness and fairness.

Just what is bothering Americans and others about the United Nations as it exists today? Can anything be done to remedy the disenchantment? What are the UN's future prospects?

In addressing these complex questions, the book is organized as follows: chapters 1 and 2 examine some of the organization's chief accomplishments and some of the criticisms leveled against it in recent years; chapters 3–5 describe the origins of the United Nations in the aftermath of World War II, the Western predominance during the organization's early years, and the rising influence of the lesser-developed, nonindustrial ("Third World") countries during the 1960s and 1970s; chapter 6 deals with the array of knotty problems facing the United Nations in the mid-1980s; chapter 7 attempts to look into the future and see where the world body may be heading during the rest of the century.

SOME REAL ACCOMPLISHMENTS

In the climate of indifference and sometimes hostility toward the United Nations that prevails in the United States in the mid-1980s, it is easy to overlook the world body's very real accomplishments. To many, all too often, including public officials and the news media, the UN headquarters on Manhattan's East River sometimes seems to have become merely a platform for verbal attacks on the United States and its allies. Positive UN activities, either behind the scenes in New York or in faraway places outside the glare of publicity, receive little or no attention. Before addressing the many complaints about the United Nations, let us look at some areas where it is unquestionably performing well and getting little credit.

PREVENTING BLOODSHED

The record of the United Nations as a supplier of peace-keeping forces may not have lived up to early expectations, but it has chalked up some notable successes. The most ambitious UN peacekeeping operation of all took place in the early 1960s, when the Congo (now Zaire) gained its independence from Belgium and quickly lapsed into near-anarchy. Bloody intertribal warfare raged, with rebellious Congolese soldiers looting, raping, and murdering European residents. As a result, Belgian troops were sent back to the former colony to restore order. The Congolese government demanded that the Belgians withdraw, and threatened to call on the Soviet Union to eject them. As all sides came to realize that such an intervention could lead to a disastrous confrontation between East and West in the heart of Africa, it was agreed to replace the Belgians with UN forces. Some twenty thousand strong, this international army took control of the disintegrating country, presided over the withdrawal of the Belgians and—persevering for years in an enormously difficult situation—helped the Congo to stand on its own feet.

Today, UN peacekeeping missions, though more modest in scope and far less dramatic than the Congo operation, are still contributing valuable service for the world community. In the Middle East, for example, three UN peacekeeping forces continue to operate despite the tremendous regional tension. The United Nations Truce Supervision Organization (UNTSO), a small group of military observers sent to the area following the Arab-Israeli war of 1948, still monitors the situation there and reports to the United Nations on potential or actual breaches of peace. The United Nations Interim Force in Lebanon (UNIFIL) was dispatched to southern Lebanon in 1978 in the hope of establishing a security zone between Israel and the guerrillas of the Palestine Liberation Organization. Neither Israel nor the PLO cooperated with the 7,000-strong international force, and the Israeli army brushed it aside when it invaded Lebanon in 1982. UNIFIL remains in Lebanon, however, and is available to help keep peace—if the political powers in the region, primarily Israel and Syria, can agree on a proper role for the UN troops. Another little-publicized example of UN peacekeeping in the Middle East is the United Nations Disengagement Observer Force (UN-DOF), a multinational group of more than a thousand men that has patrolled the buffer zone between Syria and Israel in Syria's Golan Heights since the end of the Arab-Israeli war of 1973. In this case, both sides have cooperated with UNDOF, and in June 1984 its offices were used for an exchange of prisoners.

An almost forgotten UN peacekeeping force is the United Nations Force in Cyprus (UNFICYP). Numbering approximately 2,500, it has served since 1964 to prevent a recurrence of violence between the Greek and Turkish communities on the island. At present, UNFI-CYP patrols a buffer zone between the northern (Turkish) and southern (Greek) parts of the island. It is a volatile situation: the UN presence saves lives every day by keeping the contending groups from clashing.

Even less well known to the public at large, and even more ignored by the news media, are two UN military observer groups operating along the India-Pakistan border region. These are the United Nations Military Observer Group in India and Pakistan (UNMOGIP), established in 1948, and the United Nations India-Pakistan Observer Mission (UNIPOM), initiated in 1965. India and Pakistan have fought three extremely bloody wars; the UN observers are in the region to monitor military operations and send early warning signals to the world community of any possible violations of the current peace.

In addition to those peacekeeping forces already on the job, the United Nations has been preparing to send troops to Southwest Africa (Namibia) to police a cease-fire between the Southwest Africa People's Organization (SWAPO), the chief nationalist guerrilla group, and

South Africa, the current administrator of the territory. The UN troops would also monitor elections to define the future of the country.

ALLEVIATING MISERY

The UN presence is by no means always military. With little or no fanfare, UN agencies have sent dedicated teams of workers to almost every part of the world. They may distribute food in drought-stricken African villages, care for refugees in camps along the Thai-Cambodian border, or instruct peasants in methods of sanitation in remote Andean valleys. In most instances, this humanitarian and technical work goes on without controversy— or publicity.

Created and supported chiefly by Western countries, these agencies—such as the Food and Agriculture Organization (FAO), the World Health Organization (WHO), the International Labor Organization (ILO), the United Nations Childrens Fund (UNICEF), and the Office of the High Commissioner for Refugees (UNHCR)—are doing what they can on behalf of the underprivileged of the world. UNICEF was awarded the Nobel Peace Prize in 1965 for its work to protect and educate children; the UNHCR won the Nobel Peace Prize in 1954 and 1981 for aiding the millions of people around the world who have been uprooted from their homelands and are seeking refuge elsewhere.

WHO has been responsible for many programs to improve health care around the world. Its campaign

These scientists are searching for larvae of the blackfly, the carrier of river blindness disease, in an irrigation canal in the Upper Volta region of Africa.

against river blindness is part of a major effort being made by the organization to combat tropical diseases, including malaria and leprosy, which afflict hundreds of millions of people, particularly in Asia and Africa. River blindness itself, which is thought to affect one million people, is caused by tiny parasitical worms carried by blackflies. The health organization is determined to eradicate the flies by spraying insecticide along rivers in seven African countries where the flies breed. Another major effort by WHO resulted in the worldwide eradication of smallpox. The organization's director general, Dr. Halfdan Mahler of Denmark, credits a "collective decision" by the nations of the world for the successful campaign. "In 10 years and at a cost of $100 million," says Dr. Mahler, "we were able to produce one of the great health miracles of the 20th century."

A humanitarian agency of the United Nations that has generated a good deal of criticism is the United Nations Relief and Works Agency (UNRWA). Established in 1949, this organization has made available housing, health, and education to millions of Palestinians who fled their homelands as the result of four Arab-Israeli wars. Although UNRWA undoubtedly has helped many poor, uprooted people, it has not always been possible for its field workers in Lebanon and Jordan to distinguish between nonbelligerent Palestinians and militant anti-Israeli guerrillas in distributing the agency's benefits. As a result, UN assistance has on occasion been given to gunmen instead of needy refugees.

MONITORING NUCLEAR ARMS

One of the most alarming problems faced by the United Nations, and indeed by human beings of every nationality, is the spread of nuclear technology and the proliferation of nuclear weapons. Under the aegis of the United Nations, a "Treaty on the Non-Proliferation of Nuclear Weapons" was signed in 1968. By 1982, it had been signed by 120 member states. Under the terms of the Non-Proliferation Treaty (NPT), as it is usually called, signatories agree to open their nuclear facilities to inspection by the International Atomic Energy Agency (IAEA), an organization affiliated with the United Nations. The IAEA, which reports annually to the UN General Assembly, works with the nuclear powers (the United States, the Soviet Union, Britain, France, and China) to help countries develop peaceful nuclear programs. In exchange, the agency tries to make certain that the countries do not divert fissionable materials into the development of nuclear weapons.

Some critics have argued that the IAEA's inspection system is not foolproof in that the agency cannot possibly watch over each crucial operation in the more than four dozen countries that had nuclear reactors in the mid-1980s. Countries that want to build nuclear weapons badly enough, the critics contend, will be able to hide what they are doing from the IAEA. Moreover, a number of countries capable of building nuclear weapons— among them, Argentina, Brazil, India, Israel, North Korea, Pakistan, and South Africa—have refused to sign the Non-Proliferation Treaty. This is no fault of the United Nations or the IAEA. Once again, the United Nations has provided a valuable piece of machinery; it is up to its members to use it properly.

ENCOURAGING DISARMAMENT

Since its inception, the United Nations has been a permanent forum for disarmament discussions and negotiations. It has also been the initiator of studies on the effects of nuclear weapons and fall-out, on chemical and biological weapons, on the reduction of military budgets, and on the economic and social consequences of the arms race. These UN studies show, among other things, that global military expenditures exceeded $600 billion a year during the mid-1980s. The studies pointed out that economic and social development, particularly in the poorer countries, is severely hampered by the diversion of resources into military activities.

Under consistent prodding from the United Nations, member states have reached limited but important arms-control agreements. Among them:

• the 1963 "Treaty Banning Nuclear Weapons Tests in the Atmosphere, in Outer Space and Under Water," called the Partial Test Ban Treaty because it does not ban underground tests. The General Assembly repeatedly had called for a comprehensive treaty banning all tests, whether in the atmosphere, underground or underwater.

• the 1966 "Treaty on Principles Governing the Activities of States in the Exploration and Use of Outer Space, including the Moon and Other Celestial Bodies" (Outer Space Treaty) bans nuclear and other weapons of mass destruction from the earth's orbit, prohibits the military use of celestial bodies or the placing of nuclear weapons on those bodies, and bars the stationing of weapons in outer space. The treaty, however, does not prevent nuclear weapon missiles or weapons satellites from moving through outer space; it does not ban the use of space-based platforms for launching ballistic missiles or the use of satellites to control and operate nuclear weapons.

• the 1971 "Treaty on the Prohibition of the Emplacement of Nuclear Weapons and Other Weapons of Mass Destruction on the Sea-Bed and Ocean Floor and in the Subsoil Thereof" (Sea-Bed Treaty) prohibits the placement of nuclear and other weapons of mass destruction, and facilities for such weapons, on or under the sea-bed, outside a twelve-mile coastal zone around each country. The treaty does not prohibit the installation of such weapons on mobile facilities such as submarines.

(12)

PROVIDING A
NEUTRAL TERRITORY

Another important function of the United Nations is to provide a forum in whch views can be exchanged, compromises considered, and—in some instances—results achieved. When the General Assembly convenes in September each year, an extraordinary number of presidents, prime ministers, and foreign ministers travel to UN headquarters in New York to speak before the Assembly. Their public utterances may prove stale and fruitless, but in countless quiet exchanges in the corridors, in private conference rooms or in Manhattan hotel suites, leaders from every part of the world are able to sample a range of opinion at first-hand and establish important human contacts.

This is particularly important for the countries of the Third World. Since some of them are too poor to afford embassies in every part of the world, the United Nations provides them with a unique forum for expressing their views to an international audience. For many new countries it is an extraordinary educational experience. Many are new to independence and the ways of international diplomacy. At the United Nations they are treated as sovereign states, no matter how small, backward, and powerless they may be. As member nations, they have full access to UN facilities, they may debate and discuss to their heart's content, and they can form alliances and blocs to give their voices additional influence.

It is clear, therefore, that the United Nations is providing valuable services for the world at large. To recapitulate, these services include peacekeeping operations, humanitarian and technical aid, the monitoring of nuclear arms, the encouragement of arms control, and the provision of a forum in which all points of view can be heard—accomplishments that often go unnoticed and unappreciated.

UNDER
ATTACK

Now let us examine the other side of the coin. What is causing all the sound and fury generated by critics of the United Nations? They are fierce in their attacks on its ineffectiveness and unfairness. What is the case against the United Nations?

A NEAR PARALYSIS

To begin with, there is the question of the world body's effectiveness. The primary function of the United Nations was supposed to be "keeping the peace." As mentioned in chapter 1, it has had some successes in this task. But it has had many failures. In fact, in recent years the United Nations has found itself excluded from, or on the periphery of, most crisis situations.

Secretary General Perez de Cuellar, of Peru, is well aware of this. In his first annual report to the UN General Assembly in 1982, he bluntly recited example after example of how the United Nations peacekeeping machinery has been ignored. The Peruvian cited conflicts in the Middle East between Iran and Iraq, between Israel and the allied forces of Syria and the Palestine Liberation Organization in Lebanon, and between Syria and a faction of the PLO; he referred to the bloody fighting in Afghanistan between Soviet-backed troops and Islamic guerrillas and in Cambodia between Vietnam-backed forces and a variety of rebel groups; he touched on the conflict between Ethiopia and Somalia, the civil war in Chad and the fighting between Morocco and Algeria-based guerrillas for control of the western Sahara; finally the secretary general took note of the tensions in Central America and the war between Britain and Argentina over the Falkland Islands.

In none of these disputes has the United Nations, hobbled by ideological differences and lacking consensus among its members on just what role to play, exercised significant influence. Moreover, despite some marginal achievements in the field of arms control that were mentioned in chapter 1, the United Nations has abandoned serious arms-control negotiations to the United States and the Soviet Union. "We are," Perez de Cuellar concluded, "perilously near to a new international anarchy."

The secretary general made it plain that he was not blaming this state of affairs on the United Nations as such but on the member states. As he pointed out, the office of the secretary general and the forum of the Security Council—the UN organ established to control conflict, settle disputes, and prevent wars or quickly stop them—were freely available to help in times of crisis. The trouble was, said Perez de Cuellar, that member states preferred to settle their conflicts by military force or by diplomatic means outside the United Nations.

In short, the Security Council, once considered the most powerful organ of the United Nations, has been reduced to near-paralysis. The reasons are easy to find. Chief among them is the right of the major powers on the Council to veto any resolution. The passage of a resolu-

(15)

tion in the Security Council—calling, say, for a cease-fire in a conflict or for the dispatch of peacekeeping troops— requires that nine of its fifteen members vote "yes" and that none of the five permanent members (the United States, the Soviet Union, Britain, France, and China) casts a negative vote. The veto power will be discussed elsewhere in this book, but it suffices to say at this point that the Council cannot act unless all of the so-called Big Five are in accord, and that is not a very common circumstance.

The veto, of course, has been a serious obstruction to Security Council action from the beginning of the United Nations. Despite that, until recent years the Council has been regarded as the forum most suited for serious debate by high-level representatives of parties to conflicts. At the very least, the various points of view could be aired and public attention be focused on the crisis. Today, even that modest function of the Council has been diminished. Anxious to make their voices heard on serious issues, many countries, including those with no stake at all in the disputes at hand, insist on being invited to participate in Council debate. As a result, critics argue, the Council is becoming a mini-General Assembly, where speaker after speaker is heard at enormous length, and with little or no pertinence, for the benefit of the television cameras and the audience back home. Scarce wonder that countries seeking a prompt and serious discussion of real or potential conflicts have all but given up on the Security Council.

PROPAGANDA JAMBOREE

Critics of the United Nations have other grievances. They contend that the General Assembly, once envisioned as a deliberative body in which diplomats of all member nations would weigh issues of global proportions, has become little more than an anti-Western, anti-

(16)

American jamboree. Regular sessions of the Assembly last from September to December each year, and as delegate after delegate takes to the podium the air soon thickens with intemperate attacks on the United States and its democratic allies and with extravagant praise for left-wing dictatorships.

This is hardly surprising. Many of the Third World representatives in the Assembly consider themselves Marxists of one or another form and therefore hostile to the "capitalist" (that is, Western) world. Some believe that democratic institutions as practiced by Western nations are not suitable for their own countries at their present stage of development. Still others share a conviction that their earlier domination by Western colonialism is the cause of the poverty and backwardness suffered by their countries today. In the opinion of one Western delegate, "there is kind of a Freudian element in this, an anger on the part of the newly independent countries at the old colonial 'father.' "

Given these deeply held attitudes, is it any wonder that many Third World countries are eager to heap blame on the United States, leader of the democratic Western world and the very symbol of capitalism? And is it any wonder that many of these same countries are hesitant to level the slightest criticism at Soviet actions or those of irresponsible fellow members of the Third World? Many delegates at the General Assembly may have intellectual or emotional reasons for their anti-Western, pro-Soviet utterances, but they also know that the United States displays a remarkable tolerance in the face of verbal abuse, whereas the Soviet Union is likely to find practical ways to respond to hostile remarks.

Thus we have the well-known double-standard that is applied in the General Assembly and other UN bodies. The United States is attacked by name, for example, for its intervention in Grenada. But in the matter of the Soviet invasion of Afghanistan or the Vietnamese occupation of Cambodia, it is only the presence of "foreign troops" that is deplored, since delicacy forbids pointing a finger directly at the Soviets or their Communist allies.

There are many other examples of the double standard. The United States is criticized, perhaps rightly so, for supporting antigovernment rebels in Nicaragua, but not one word is said about Libyan intervention in Chad in behalf of rebel forces. In speech after speech, Israel and the United States are censured for retaining trade ties with South Africa, the land of apartheid. It does not even embarrass these speakers that their own governments maintain trade ties with the white supremacists. For example, forty-nine African countries, most of them black, engaged in trade with South Africa in 1983. According to the International Monetary Fund, in 1984 the Soviet Union and its Eastern bloc allies, who are among the loudest critics of U.S. and Israeli policies, were also conducting a growing trade with South Africa.

THE ISRAELI WHIPPING BOY

In recent years, the favorite target for criticism and abuse at the United Nations has been Israel. And in the view of many observers, there have been legitimate reasons to complain of Israel's behavior on occasion. With the exception of the Sinai Peninsula, which it returned to Egypt, Israel steadfastly has refused to give up the territories it seized in the 1967 war with the Arabs. It has continued to expand its settlements in conquered Arab lands on the West Bank of the Jordan and in the Gaza Strip, actions repeatedly condemned by countries of every political stripe, including the United States, as an illegal form of "creeping annexation." The Israeli invasion of Lebanon in 1982 and the heavy toll it took on civilian life also led to harsh criticism at the United Nations and attempts to strip Israel of its membership in various UN bodies, including the International Atomic

Energy Agency and the International Telecommunications Union. The attempts were blocked by Western opposition.

But if Israel's conduct has been subject to question at times, so has that of many other countries. The difference is they escape unscathed by UN resolutions, whereas Israel has been attacked by name in literally hundreds of them. On many occasions, it has appeared that the Third World majority in the General Assembly, egged on by the Soviet Union, has gone out of its way to offend Israel and its friends. In 1974, Yasir Arafat, then the unchallenged leader of the Palestine Liberation Organization and leader of its terrorist war against Israel, was invited to address the Assembly. After speaking with a pistol holster showing beneath his jacket, the guerrilla chieftain was given a standing ovation by the delegates. Soon after, the Assembly further enraged the Israelis by granting "observer status" to the PLO, thus placing it on the same footing as Switzerland and the Vatican.

In a calculated affront, the Assembly outraged the Israelis and others in 1975, when it passed by a large majority a resolution branding Zionism, the Jewish nationalist movement that led to the formation of the state of Israel, as a "form of racism and racial discrimination." In 1982, the Assembly condemned Israel as a "non-peace-loving state"—the first member ever to be so indicted. The condemnation might have led to Israel's expulsion from the Assembly, but that was prevented when the United States threatened to pick up its money bags and follow Israel out the door. Militant Arab spokesmen, however, have made it clear that they will continue their efforts to expel Israel from the General Assembly. Israel still takes part in all major United Nations bodies, but it rules out a major role for the United Nations in Middle East diplomacy, convinced that it cannot get a fair deal in the organization that gave it birth in 1948.

Israeli delegates to the UN were enraged by the courtesies extended to PLO leader Yasir Arafat, shown here addressing the General Assembly, during his 1974 visit to the UN.

BUDGETS, BUREAUCRATS,
AND ESPIONAGE AGENTS

If critics of the United Nations have trained their heaviest guns on the breakdown of the Security Council and the conversion of the General Assembly and some of the specialized agencies into sterile propaganda forums, they also have a long list of complaints about the Secretariat itself. The United States, which foots 25 percent of the Secretariat's annual budget of approximately $750 million,* and up to a third of the combined $4.7 billion annual budget of the specialized agencies, has frequently complained of excessive spending by the world body. This view is shared by other major contributors. In 1982, the U.S. ambassador, joined by those of Britain and the Soviet Union, marched upstairs to the office of Secretary General Perez de Cuellar and delivered a strong protest against out-of-control spending. The secretary general promised to do his best, but in fact his hands are tied. His office does indeed propose a budget each year, but there is no budget ceiling at the United Nations. The Third World majority, many of whose members typically pay only one or two ten-thousandths of the budget, blithely endorses additional programs that add to the cost of running the organization. As one Western diplomat put it, "the Secretary General proposes, and the Third World disposes."

Another subject of concern and annoyance to cost-conscious critics is the salary level of Secretariat employees, who typically earn about 35 percent more than comparable U.S. civil servants. The critics also allege that

---

*The Soviet Union pays roughly 12 percent, Japan pays a little over 10 percent, Western Europe's nineteen members pay a total of 39 percent, and the remaining amount—around 14 percent—is shared among the organization's remaining 137 members. Members' assessments are based on their ability to pay.

many of the UN staffers are unproductive bureaucrats who churn out masses of unreadable and unread documents. This may be arguable, but it is fact that each year the United Nations circulates close to eight thousand separate reports as official documents. Stacking one copy of each report upon another would create a tower of paper 120 feet high. A preliminary estimate indicated that the number of pages of documents the United Nations would print in 1984 would reach 1.1 billion.

Still another serious criticism of the UN Secretariat concerns its personnel practices. As already pointed out, employees of the Secretariat are supposed to be international civil servants, men and women who remain impartial in international questions and owe allegiance first and foremost to the world body itself. In practice, this has been impossible to enforce. It is widely accepted at the United Nations that most Western members of the Secretariat staff are truly private citizens; they do not represent their countries or the governments in power in those countries, and they are not nominated by them for posts at the United Nations. On the other hand, all Secretariat personnel from Communist-bloc countries, and from many Third World states, are provided by their governments and are expected to carry out their governments' instructions. These countries simply do not accept the concept, perhaps a naive one, of an independent, objective international civil service. At United Nations headquarters in New York, the Soviet diplomats attached to the Soviet mission to the United Nations do not even disguise their view that their countrymen who are members of the Secretariat staff are Soviets first and UN employees second. Each one is expected to attend frequent meetings at the Soviet mission and feed it information gained in the Secretariat. This practice is strictly contrary to the UN Charter, but it has been tolerated as a matter of expediency.

This leads to the subject of espionage. Since the Soviet members of the Secretariat staff are supplied by the Moscow government, it is not surprising that UN headquarters in New York and UN offices elsewhere are heavily infiltrated by agents of the Soviet Union's primary intelligence agency, the KGB. It is quite possible that Western nations, including the United States, have also planted espionage agents in the UN Secretariat, but if so, no hint of it has surfaced. On the other hand, there have been documented cases, buttressed by the testimony of Soviet defectors, of KGB agents occupying high positions in the Secretariat. Top UN officials will admit as much, but they play down the importance of the infiltration and maintain that the confidentiality of Secretariat information is not jeopardized. "The Soviets are frozen out," a senior Secretariat official claims. "Nobody tells them anything—unless, for example, they want something leaked to the Soviet government."

Still, many critics are not happy with a situation in which Soviet intelligence operatives—in a word, spies—hold top positions in the UN Secretariat. Clearly, this is not what the early supporters of the United Nations had in mind.

BOLD NEW EXPERIMENT

For centuries, thinkers and dreamers have proposed schemes for maintaining international peace, order, and justice. But not until the twentieth century, as a consequence of two great wars of unprecedented horror and destruction, has mankind actually been able to construct organizations designed to bring harmony to the conflicting policies and actions of nations. The first of these organizations, the League of Nations, was formed in the aftermath of World War I and collapsed when it failed to prevent the even greater calamity of World War II. The United Nations, an offspring of World War II, is still with us after four difficult, dangerous decades.

FAILURE OF THE LEAGUE

Americans played leading roles in the formation of both international organizations. On January 8, 1918, while shells still screamed into the blood-soaked trenches of Europe, U.S. president Woodrow Wilson appeared before Congress and delivered his famous Fourteen Points address. For the most part, the speech was a statement of Wilson's idealistic war aims, including such "points" as the abolition of secret diplomacy and self-determination for various ethnic groups. But the president regarded the fourteenth point—calling for the formation of a League of Nations "to secure mutual guarantees of political independence and territorial integrity to great and small nations alike"—to be of central importance.

After Germany's surrender in November 1918, the world—at least most of the Western world—wondered whether Wilson's vision of a world organization could be put into practice. In January 1919, the victorious Allied leaders, President Wilson of the United States, Prime Minister Lloyd George of Britain, Premier Clemenceau of France, and Premier Orlando of Italy met in Paris to fashion a peace treaty with Germany. Part of the treaty was to be a Covenant of the League of Nations, and Wilson was appointed chairman of the committee to draft it. Spurred on by the president, the committee produced a draft in less than two weeks. Proclaimed Wilson: "A living thing is born."

But if the League was indeed born, its father's country was soon to disown it. To Wilson's enormous distress, the U.S. Senate rejected American membership in the organization as the country's traditional position of isolation from world affairs reasserted itself after the heady wartime intervention in Europe. Typical was the comment of one U.S. diplomat: "Damned well out of that European mess!"

Crippled from the start without the participation of the world's most powerful country, the League survived the 1920s but could not head off the storm that appeared in the 1930s. It was unable to prevent the Japanese conquest of Manchuria in 1931, Italian dictator Benito Mussolini's seizure of Ethiopia in 1935, the illegal rearmament of Germany under Adolf Hitler, or Germany's

(25)

reoccupation of the Rhineland in 1936 in violation of the Versailles Treaty ending World War I. The dictators appeared to be unstoppable. While Britain and France tried to appease them, the United States watched with seeming indifference from behind its Atlantic and Pacific moats. Finally, the aggressions of Nazi Germany and its Italian and Japanese allies forced the world into the bloodiest struggle in history. World War II, which lasted from 1939 to 1945 and took at least 34 million lives, was the final nail in the coffin of Woodrow Wilson's impotent offspring, the League of Nations.

LOOKING AHEAD

After the Japanese attack on Pearl Harbor on December 7, 1941, the United States entered World War II as an ally of Britain, China, and the Soviet Union* against the Axis powers of Germany, Italy, and Japan. Two weeks later, British prime minister Winston Churchill arrived in Washington for talks with President Franklin Roosevelt and other Allied leaders. The result was the historic "Declaration by the United Nations," pledging the twenty-six signatory nations to a unified struggle against the common enemy. This was the first public use of the term "United Nations," a phrase usually attributed to President Roosevelt.

The Declaration of the United Nations was an event of enormous importance in U.S. diplomatic history. Not only did it constitute a rallying cry for an all-out effort to defeat the Axis powers; it also provided the embryo of a new world organization for peace. Though the Declaration marked a radical departure from America's traditional policies of isolation and nonentanglement in for-

---

*At the time, France was not part of the alliance. Part of it was occupied by the Germans, the rest of it was in the hands of a German-dominated government located in the city of Vichy—the so-called "Vichy government."

eign alliances, it was received enthusiastically by the people of the United States.

It was generally accepted by the Allied leaders that once the war was won, an entirely new world organization would have to be built. The League of Nations, fairly or unfairly, reeked with the odor of failure. In the United States, political leaders were convinced that it would be far better to try to enlist public support for a new organization than to revive the stale and fruitless controversy over the failure of the United States to enter the League of Nations.

Roosevelt and his Democratic administration realized that they would have to prepare the people of the United States for a postwar peace organization even while they fought the war in Europe and Asia. The partisan split that took place between Democrats and Republicans over entry into the League of Nations had to be avoided. So, in 1942, Secretary of State Cordell Hull established an Advisory Committee on Postwar Foreign Policy. The committee, including influential Republicans as well as Democrats, pledged its support to the establishment of an international organization for peace. The House of Representatives, by an overwhelming vote of 360 to 29, rejected isolationist arguments and expressed its support for American participation in such an organization.

BUILDING THE FOUNDATION

Another major step toward the foundation of the United Nations organization was taken on October 30, 1943, in the "Moscow Declaration of the Four Nations on General Security." In it, the Big Four of the United States, the Soviet Union, Britain, and China announced that "they recognize the need to establish at the earliest practicable date a general international organization, based on the principle of the sovereign equality of all peace-loving states, and open to membership of all such states, large or small, for the maintenance of international peace and security."

During 1943 and 1944, as it became clear that the Axis powers would be defeated, Allied leaders were giving hard thought to the nature of the postwar world. In July 1944, the United Nations Monetary and Financial Conference, including a small army of twelve hundred experts, met in the fashionable Bretton Woods resort in the mountains of New Hampshire. There the representatives of forty-four nations took part in lengthy discussions and finally came up with an agreement of a two-pronged plan. The first part established an International Monetary Fund of $8.8 billion to make loans that would help countries stabilize their currencies, remedy their trade deficits, and generally stimulate trade. The second prong was a World Bank capitalized at $9.1 billion to make loans to needy countries for reconstruction and development projects. (The treaties creating the Fund and the Bank were finally ratified at Quebec in December 1945 after a sufficient number of countries accepted the terms.)

The political counterpart of the Bretton Woods Conference convened at Dumbarton Oaks, a spacious estate in the Georgetown section of Washington, D.C., on August 21, 1944 and lasted until October 7. During those weeks, the representatives of the United States, the Soviet Union, Britain, and China hammered together a tentative draft of a charter for a new world organization. It provided for an Assembly, in which all "peace-loving states" would be represented and have one vote apiece. It also envisaged a Security Council, which would bear chief responsibility for maintaining peace and security in the world. The major powers—the United States, the Soviet Union, Britain, China, and a postwar, liberated France—would be given special weight on the Council, it was agreed; but the conferees failed to resolve fully the problem posed by the Soviet insistence that each of the great powers have a veto over *all* decisions of the Council.

In February 1945, with Germany collapsing and Japan reeling, Roosevelt met with British leader Churchill and Soviet leader Joseph Stalin at Yalta, a resort on the Crimean peninsula of the Soviet Union. France was not represented because it was not yet liberated from the Germans, and China was not at Yalta because the main item on the agenda concerned the treatment of the soon-to-be defeated European enemies in such areas as occupation policy, reparations, and punishment. Also of prime importance to the three leaders was the historic task of restructuring the political map of much of central Europe for the postwar world. But the conferees also found time for the question of the United Nations. In a decision that would prove to be of long-lasting importance, the United States and Britain accepted the Soviet position on the Security Council—or what they understood it to be. Except on purely procedural matters, each of the major powers would have a veto power over all decisions. The three leaders then agreed that all members of the United Nations should convene in San Francisco on April 25, 1945, to draft the final charter of the organization. It was further agreed that China and France, along with the Big Three, would be invited to act as sponsoring governments of the San Francisco conference.

Addressing the U.S. Congress on his return from Yalta, President Roosevelt declared, "This time we shall not make the mistake of waiting until the end of the war to set up the machinery of peace. This time, as we fight together to get the war over quickly, we work together to keep it from happening again." In preparing for the San Francisco conference, Roosevelt took pains to avoid the partisan political wrangling that led to the U.S. rejection of the League of Nations. The American delegation would be scrupulously nonpartisan: four Democrats, three Republicans and one independent Democrat.

MEETING IN SAN FRANCISCO

Preparations for the San Francisco conference were proceeding smoothly when Roosevelt suddenly died on April 12, less than two weeks before the opening session. But within an hour after his succession to the presidency, Harry S. Truman announced that the conference would be held on schedule. With flags flapping at half-mast in honor of Roosevelt, the historic meeting began on April 25. Representatives of forty-six countries (ultimately fifty by the end of the conference) took their seats in the San Francisco Opera House with the awareness that mankind had been given a second chance to build an organization that would secure peace, order, and justice in the world.

The beginning of the conference was far from auspicious. The war in Europe and Asia was still raging, but the wartime unity between the Soviet Union and the Western allies was beginning to dissolve. In mid-March, the Soviet Union had already made it clear that it was transforming Poland and Romania into Communist satellites in violation of solemn pledges made at Yalta that democratic elections would be held. In April, the American army was dashing across Germany, in excellent position to capture its capital of Berlin and also seize Prague, the capital of Czechoslovakia. Instead, American military strategists, presumably to save American lives, permitted Soviet troops to conquer these ancient capitals and establish Soviet power deep in the heart of central Europe. That decision proved to be one of the most fateful of the twentieth century, since it permitted the Communist rulers in Moscow to extend their sway far beyond their borders and construct an iron sphere of influence that exists until this day. Quite clearly, history was being made not only at San Francisco but in far-off battlefields where military might was establishing the new political realities. On the very day the conference opened, Soviet

(30)

troops surrounded Berlin and prepared for an entry into the shattered city.

As a consequence of these momentous events, and of the growing awareness that the postwar world would not be one of cooperation but confrontation between the Western powers and the Soviet Union, the atmosphere at San Francisco was one of tension and suspicion. Invoking a secret agreement made at Yalta, the Soviet Union insisted that it be given additional seats at the conference in the name of Byelorussia and the Ukraine, two of its "republics" (comparable to American states). After some debate, the two extra seats were granted. But when the Soviet Union demanded that Moscow's hand-picked Communist government in Poland be given a seat, the conferees flatly refused.

From then on, East and West were at each other's throats, arguing vehemently about point after point in the UN Charter to which they were trying to give birth. Perhaps the most crucial controversy arose over the question of the major power veto in the Security Council. Supposedly this problem had been resolved by Roosevelt, Churchill, and Stalin at Yalta, but when smaller powers led by Australia and New Zealand questioned the concept of the veto, it quickly became apparent that the Western powers and the Soviet Union had different views on what had been agreed upon at Yalta.

It is important to be clear about the dispute over the veto, since it later came to assume such importance in discussions about the United Nations and its inability to act decisively. Not only the Soviet Union, but the Western powers—the United States, Britain, and France—insisted on the veto power in the Security Council. In fact, Filipino statesman Carlos Romulo, one of the delegates at San Francisco, later recalled that U.S. Secretary of State Edward Stettinius told him the United States would not join the United Nations without having the veto. But the United States and its allies were willing to limit the veto power to matters of substance, while the Soviet Union insisted that the Big Three had agreed to a 100 percent veto power at Yalta. This would mean that the veto would apply to *all* matters in the Security Council, including procedural matters such as what questions the Council could put on its agenda and who could take part in debate. The Western powers opposed this, as did the smaller powers, who branded the 100 percent veto an attempt by the Soviet Union at "gag rule."

The acute crisis created by this dispute seemed to endanger the whole conference. The deadlock was broken only after President Truman made a personal appeal to Stalin and the Soviet dictator softened his stand. As a result, the great powers would retain their veto in the Council on all questions of substance—for instance, a conflict between member states, a call for member states to settle their differences, or the establishment of a UN peacekeeping force. On strictly procedural matters, including the right of small states to bring matters before the Council for debate, the veto would not pertain. Thus every member would be able to be heard in what was envisaged as the strongest organ of the United Nations.

Once this obstacle was overcome, the major problems of the conference were over, and by June the delegates cleared away last-minute logjams and concluded their labors. President Truman flew to San Francisco to congratulate the diplomats, and on June 25, exactly two months after the opening session, they unanimously approved their own handiwork. The formal signing of the leather-bound Charter Book took place the next day. The United Nations officially came into existence on October 24, 1945, after the Charter had been ratified by China, France, the Soviet Union, Great Britain, and the United States and by a majority of the other signatories. October 24 is celebrated each year as "United Nations Day."

*U.S. Secretary of State Edward Stettinius
signing the official Charter; a pleased
President Harry Truman stands at the left.*

THE NEW ORGANIZATION

The preamble to the United Nations Charter reads in part: "We the peoples of the United Nations . . . determined to save succeeding generations from the scourge of war, which twice in our lifetime has brought untold sorrow to mankind . . . do hereby establish an international organization to be known as the United Nations." In the hope of eliminating war and of bettering the lot of mankind in other ways, the Charter established six principal organs of the United Nations: the General Assembly, the Security Council, the Economic and Social Council, the Trusteeship Council, the International Court of Justice and a Secretariat headed by a secretary general.

• *General Assembly.* The main deliberative body, the Assembly is composed of representatives of all member states, each of which has the same rights and one vote, irrespective of size, population, or wealth. On most issues decisions are made by majority vote. In the case of "important questions," such as recommendations on peace and security, admission of new members and budgetary matters, a two-thirds majority is required. The Assembly may consider any international problem that two-thirds of its members deem fit to be on the agenda. But in spite of attempts over the years to expand the powers of the Assembly, it can only *recommend* actions or remedies in any given situation; it cannot adopt resolutions that have binding legal force for member governments. The General Assembly does have power to consider and approve the annual budget of the United Nations and apportion contributions to that budget by member nations.

• *Security Council.* Under the Charter, the Security Council has the primary responsibility for the maintenance of international peace and security. It has fifteen members: five permanent ones—the United States, the Soviet Union, Britain, France, and China—and ten elected by the General Assembly for two-year terms. Decisions on procedural matters are made by a "yes" vote of at least nine of the fifteen; decisions on substantive matters require nine yes votes, including the yes or "abstain" votes of *all* five permanent members. This is the great power veto. Thus, no resolution on an issue of substance can be passed against the wishes of any of the permanent members of the Council.

The Council alone has the power to make decisions which member states are obligated to carry out under the Charter. The Council can determine the existence of a threat to the peace or an act of aggression and then decide what action should be taken. It can call on member states to apply economic sanctions to prevent or stop aggression. It can call for and actually carry out collective military action against an aggressor. These Charter-given powers would make the Security Council a potent body—if it were not for the veto, which guarantees that only those actions agreed upon by the five major powers can be acted upon.

- *Economic and Social Council.* In response to demands by the smaller powers at San Francisco, the framers of the Charter established the Economic and Social Council (ECOSOC) as the central body for the discussion and investigation of economic and social matters. As such, it considers a wide range of issues and coordinates the activities of the "specialized agencies"*— sometimes known as the UN's "family" of organizations.

---

*A number of important UN-affiliated bodies are not categorized as specialized agencies, chiefly because they report to the General Assembly rather than to ECOSOC. These include the International Atomic Energy Agency (IAEA), the United Nations Children's Fund (UNICEF), and the United Nations Development Program (UNDP).

The network of specialized agencies, which report annually to the Economic and Social Council, is made up of the following:

- International Labor Organization (ILO)
- Food and Agriculture Organization (FAO)
- United Nations Educational, Scientific and Cultural Organization (UNESCO)
- World Health Organization (WHO)
- World Bank/International Bank for Reconstruction and Development (IBRD)
- International Development Association (IDA)
- International Finance Corporation (IFC)
- International Monetary Fund (IMF)
- International Civil Aviation Organization (ICAO)
- Universal Postal Union (UPU)
- International Telecommunication Union (ITU)
- World Meteorological Organization (WMO)
- International Maritime Organization (IMO)
- World Intellectual Property Organization (WIPO)
- International Fund for Agricultural Development (IFAD)

It is important to note that each of these specialized agencies operates under its own constitution and enjoys considerable autonomy. Membership varies, since only those member states that choose to participate are represented in each organization.

- *Trusteeship Council.* After World War I, the League of Nations originated the "mandate system." Instead of the victors openly dividing up the colonies of defeated Germany, Austria-Hungary, and Turkey, they were given mandates by the League to administer those territories for the benefit of the inhabitants. For example, Britain became the mandate power in Palestine, France in

Syria, South Africa in South-West Africa, Australia in New Guinea, and the United States in a number of Pacific islands. After World War II and the formation of the United Nations, all except one* of the mandated territories were placed under a UN system of trusteeship.

Under this system, the Trusteeship Council was assigned the task of supervising the administration of the trust territories. The major objective of the Council was to promote the advancement of the inhabitants of the trust territories and their development toward self-government and independence.

The powers of the Trusteeship Council are threefold. The first is the right to submit questionnaires to the administering powers and receive reports from them. The second is the right to accept petitions from the people of the trust territories and examine them in consultation with the administering powers. The third is the right to visit the territories at times agreed upon with the administering authorities.

The major objective of the Council has been fulfilled to such an extent that all but one of the original eleven trusteeships have gained independence, either as separate states or by joining neighboring independent countries. Only the Trust Territory of Pacific Islands, administered by the United States, remains in a state of dependency.

• *International Court of Justice.* Popularly known as the World Court, this is the principal judicial organ of the United Nations. The various UN organs may ask the

---

*South Africa refused to place South-West Africa under the UN trusteeship system. The move generated much dispute, and in 1950 the World Court ruled that South Africa had not acted illegally. The court held, however, that South Africa was obliged to present to the United Nations the same kind of reports it rendered to the League. South Africa has refused to do so, despite many UN resolutions condemning its conduct. See the Namibia question, pp. 78–80.

Court for advisory opinions on any legal question, but the United Nations cannot bring cases before the court for litigation. Only member countries may be parties to actual suits in the World Court. Moreover, each member country decides whether or not it will accept the jurisdiction of the Court. And even when a country has accepted the jurisdiction of the Court, it is permitted to do so with reservations of its own making, either about the subject matter it will allow the Court to adjudicate or, more sweepingly, about matters considered to be solely within its domestic jurisdiction.

The Court consists of fifteen judges elected by the General Assembly and the Security Council, voting independently. In theory, they are selected on the basis of their qualifications, not on the basis of nationality. No two judges can be nationals of the same country, and care is taken to insure that the principal legal systems of the world are represented. Judges serve for a period of nine years. Unlike the General Assembly, the Security Council, the Economic and Social Council, and the Trusteeship Council, all of which are headquartered in New York, the World Court has its seat at The Hague, Netherlands.

• *Secretariat.* As pointed out in the Introduction, the Secretariat services the other organs of the United Nations and administers the programs and policies laid down by them. According to the Charter, members of the Secretariat are international civil servants, obliged to work for the world body and not for particular governments. This ideal situation, however, does not always prevail.

At the head of the Secretariat is the secretary general, who is chosen by the General Assembly but only on the recommendation of the Security Council. In effect, this means that the secretary general is really picked by the Council, where the veto is in effect and where any of the five permanent members can turn thumbs down on any given candidate. In addition to being the "chief administrative officer of the Organization," the Charter also endows him with a political role. He may, for instance, bring to the attention of the Security Council any matter which in his opinion may threaten the maintenance of international peace and security. In addition, the secretary general may make the widest possible range of recommendations to the General Assembly in his annual report to that body. On an informal level, the secretary general may also use his good offices to help solve international disputes.

The organization forged at San Francisco did not satisfy everyone at the time, and it certainly does not satisfy everyone today. But given the state of the world in 1945, with its conflicting ideologies and ambitions, with the suspicions and bitterness displayed by the chief participants, the organization may have been the best achievable. Whatever the weaknesses of the United Nations Charter, the delegates at San Francisco established the machinery for the boldest experiment in international organization yet conceived by man.

EARLY
YEARS

The United Nations was officially launched in January 1946, when the General Assembly and the Security Council convened for the first time in London. There the infant organization quickly learned that lingering hopes for cooperation among the wartime allies were indeed pipe dreams. From the start, it was East (the Soviet Union and its Communist allies) against West (the United States, Western Europe and their allies). They clashed over petty organizational matters and over the naming of the first secretary general. The West favored either Lester Pearson of Canada or Eelco van Kleffens of the Netherlands, while the Soviet bloc supported Yugoslavia's Stanoje Simic. After much debate, a compromise was reached, and the choice for this important post was the foreign minister of Norway, Trygve Lie.

GLOBAL CONFLICT

The early difficulties of the United Nations were not merely the inevitable birth pangs of a new organization.

The world clearly was embarked on an epochal political struggle, and nowhere was that struggle more evident than in central Europe, where the Soviet Union had slammed down an Iron Curtain between its Communist satellites of Eastern Europe and the democracies of Western Europe. Trygve Lie, a blunt labor leader turned diplomat, would soon feel the heat-generated by the East-West conflict.

On January 19, 1946, the Security Council received its first complaint. It came from Iran and charged that Soviet troops, which had occupied the oil-rich Iranian province of Azerbaijan during World War II, refused to withdraw despite agreements between the two governments. The Iranians also complained about Soviet interference in their internal affairs. The Soviets were, or pretended to be, incensed. Whenever the issue was raised in the Security Council, the Soviet delegate stalked out of the chamber. At this early stage, the Council—faced with the implicit threat of a Soviet veto—was unable to act. As a result, Soviet troops remained in Azerbaijan until they established a puppet Communist state in the province. Once the Soviet soldiers left, the Iranian government obliterated the government they left behind; but the whole episode was the first example of how powerless the Security Council could be when it was faced by the intransigence of one of its permanent members.

The location of the permanent headquarters of the United Nations was the subject of intense discussion among the diplomats gathered in London. Some argued for a site in Europe, since this was where two world wars had started and where the world body would have to watch closely for signs of a third. Others contended that an American headquarters was necessary in order to retain American interest and prevent a return to isolationism. In the end, most countries agreed that Manhattan island, in New York City, with its unrivaled telecommunications facilities and its location in the hub of financial power and cultural activity, would be the ideal location. The selection of Manhattan was clinched when John D. Rockefeller, Jr., offered the United Nations a gift of $8.5 million to buy a strip of land along the East River at a location known as Turtle Bay.

The gift was promptly accepted by the General Assembly, the land was acquired and the construction of the UN headquarters begun. Not until 1951–1952 was the impressive 39-story glass Secretariat building and the low-domed Conference building ready for occupancy. In the meantime, temporary quarters were found, first at Hunter College in the Bronx, then at a converted skating rink in Queens, and later at a former Sperry Gyroscope factory in the suburban New York village of Lake Success. The name of the latter site proved to be ironic, for the years spent there were a very mixed success at best. Time and time again, the Soviet Union used its veto power in the Security Council, blocking the passage of resolutions and badly crippling that body. It had been hoped in the West that the veto would be used sparingly by the major powers, and never to obstruct procedure or choke off debate. But the Soviet Union, then outnumbered by the non-Communist countries, made up for its numerical inferiority by wielding the veto ruthlessly and regularly.

ATOMIC WEAPONS

Of particular dismay to the West was the Soviet attitude, as expressed at the United Nations, toward the international control of atomic weapons. During the early years of the world body's existence, the United States still retained a monopoly on atomic arms. Nevertheless, in 1946 President Truman offered to turn over the secret and control of this terrible new weapon to the United Nations. In the so-called "Baruch Plan" (named after the financier and philanthropist Bernard Baruch, who presented it to the United Nations), the United States proposed that the world body establish an International

Atomic Development Authority which would firmly monitor the world's production of atomic energy.

If established, the authority would have had exclusive control over all atomic activities, from the mining of raw materials to the use of fissionable fuel. Under this incredibly far-reaching plan, the United Nations would have owned and managed all uranium and thorium mines, refineries, chemical separation plants, and reactors, and would have had the exclusive right to engage in atomic research. As if that were not extraordinary enough, the Baruch Plan also envisaged that the Authority—operating without the interference of a great power veto—would have the power to punish nations that violated atomic energy agreements. To make certain that the Authority really exercised total control over atomic energy, the U.S. plan would have given it the right to make on-site inspections in any country in the world. Said one diplomat at the time: "It was the most far-reaching and dramatic proposal for supranational authority that any government has ever presented anywhere; it amounted to world government in a very important field of human activity."

It may have been questionable whether this remarkable plan would have been acceptable to the U.S. Congress, but the world was never given a chance to find out. The Soviet Union immediately denounced the proposal as "thoroughly vicious and unacceptable." For one thing, the Soviets, then as now, were totally unwilling to allow inspectors from other nations to prowl around their homeland. Besides, the Russians could not accept the idea that the United States, even though it turned over its atomic secrets to the United Nations, would still be the only country on earth with the knowledge to make atomic weapons. The Soviet Union's growing pride demanded that it, too, make bombs before renunciation of them could be discussed. By 1949, the Russians succeeded in creating their own atomic bomb. Hopes for UN control over the new weapons now were dashed and the nuclear arms race was on in earnest. Down the road lay the development of the hydrogen bomb, intercontinental missiles, tactical and intermediate nuclear missiles, and preparations for nuclear warfare in space.

ISRAEL IS BORN

While the Security Council was falling victim to the increasingly bitter conflict between East and West, which came to be known as the Cold War, the General Assembly displayed occasional fits of vitality. One such occasion concerned Palestine and the British mandate over that troubled land. As mentioned earlier (page 36), Britain had been given the right to administer Palestine by the League of Nations after World War I.

When Britain assumed its role as mandatory power in 1920, Arabs made up nearly 90 percent of the population. But during the 1920s and 1930s, Jewish immigration increased sharply—encouraged and financed by various Zionist (Jewish nationalist) organizations. Some of the Jewish settlers came legally; many others came illegally, circumventing British attempts to control the flow of immigration. As the number of Jewish settlements and institutions multiplied, resentment against Zionism, the Jews, and the British flared among the Arabs of Palestine. Violence between Arabs and Jews, and by both against the British, mounted steadily during and after World War II. Finally, Britain—exhausted by its efforts in World War II and fed up with the strife in Palestine—dumped its burden on the doorstep of the UN General Assembly in 1947.

For the General Assembly, still in its infancy, the Palestine question was a major one to confront. The Jews had long dreamed of returning to their ancestral homeland and establishing a state where they would be free from the persecution that had hounded them through the centuries. And after the murder of six million Jews by the Nazis during the 1930s and 1940s, the Zionists were more determined than ever to achieve their goal. The Arabs, on the other hand, had been the majority people of Palestine for over a thousand years. Even after the waves of Zionist immigrants moved into Palestine during the years of the British mandate, Arabs outnumbered Jews in the Holy Land by at least two to one when Britain turned to the United Nations.

For months the General Assembly debated the issue and in the end—heavily influenced by the United States and the Western powers—came to a decision that was cheered by the Zionists and denounced by the Arabs. The land of Palestine would be partitioned between Arabs and Jews; the city of Jerusalem would be internationalized and placed under the control of the United Nations. On May 14, 1948, in accord with the Assembly's decision, the Zionists announced the formation of the new state of Israel.

As a result of the partition, grave trouble was in store for the Middle East. Less than twenty-four hours after the establishment of Israel, the Arab armies of Egypt, Jordan, Syria, Iraq, and Lebanon invaded the newborn state. In the fighting that followed, Israel repelled the invaders. But it was only the first of four full-fledged Arab-Israeli wars, not to mention countless acts of violence, that were to plague the Middle East. Millions of Palestinian Arabs were to become refugees scattered throughout the Arab world and beyond. Israel was to push its borders far beyond those delineated by the United Nations. As of the mid-1980s, most of the Arab world was still bitterly hostile to Israel and the Palestine question was very much on the world body's agenda.

At the time, however, Britain's decision to call on the General Assembly to determine the future of Palestine greatly enhanced that body's prestige. By making use of the Assembly to deal with a major political matter, all parties concerned allowed that body to operate in an area the framers of the Charter intended to reserve for the Security Council. The British move was one of the ear-

(45)

liest Western attempts to get around the Council, with its hobbling veto, and look to the Assembly, where the West then had a decided numerical advantage.

THE COLD WAR HEIGHTENS

During 1947 and 1948, the struggle between the Western democracies and the Communist bloc intensified. To head off takeovers by Communist guerrillas in Greece and Turkey, President Truman asked Congress to appropriate $400 million for economic and military aid to those countries, a request that was granted. This was the beginning of the historic "Truman Doctrine," a new American policy which pledged support for "free peoples who are resisting attempted subjugation by armed minorities or by outside pressures." As American aid reached Greece and Turkey, these two countries grew strong enough to successfully fight off the Communists.

The Cold War was further heightened in January 1948, when Communists staged a *coup d'état* in Czechoslovakia, overthrowing the democratically elected government and murdering Foreign Minister Jan Masaryk. Determined to stem the Western advance of Communism and help postwar Western Europe to its feet, President Truman took another major step by launching the "Marshall Plan." Named after his secretary of state, George C. Marshall, this bold initiative would pump a $12 billion economic transfusion into the European democracies over a four-year period. In doing so, the United States helped create economic and social conditions in which the free people of Western Europe could practice democratic free choice.

Inasmuch as the United Nations, and particularly the veto-bound Security Council, was shackled as a protector against aggression, the Western European democracies looked to their own defenses against the huge armed forces massed by the Communist bloc in Eastern Europe. In March 1948, Britain, France, the Netherlands, Belgium, and Luxembourg signed the Brussels Pact, a five-year defense treaty binding the parties to aid one another in the event of an attack by an aggressor. Later that year, the United States indicated its interest in joining the anti-Communist alliance, and on April 4, 1949, representatives of twelve Western nations—the United States, Canada, Britain, France, Italy, Belgium, the Netherlands, Luxembourg, Norway, Denmark, Iceland, and Portugal—met in Washington to form the North Atlantic Treaty Organization (NATO).* In the pact, the signatories stipulated that an attack on one would be regarded as an attack on all—a clear signal to Moscow that it must curb its ambitions.

In Asia, too, Communism seemed to be on the march. In 1949, the Communist armies of Mao Tse-tung defeated the Nationalists led by Chiang Kai-shek and forced them to flee the Chinese mainland and set up an exile government on the offshore island of Taiwan. At the time, the new Chinese government in Beijing (formerly Peking) was firmly allied with the Soviet Union, and together the two Communist giants seemed a formidable threat to the Western democracies and their allies in every part of the world.

All these epochal events could not but have an adverse effect on proceedings at the United Nations. The interests of the Western democracies and those of the Communist world were so profoundly opposed that debate in UN bodies became boringly antagonistic and totally unproductive. Secretary General Trygve Lie did his best to maintain an impartial stance, but in the end this proved impossible.

THE KOREAN CRISIS

Such was the international atmosphere in 1950, when the young world organization was faced with its severest test

---

*Greece and Turkey were to join later.

to date. The year began with a Soviet proposal to remove the representative of Nationalist China from his seat on the Security Council on the grounds that the Communist government in Beijing actually represented the people of China. The defeat of this proposal led to a Soviet boycott of the Security Council and all other UN organs.

Shortly thereafter, on June 25, word arrived at the United Nations that South Korea, an American ally, had been invaded by a Soviet-trained, Soviet-equipped, and presumably Soviet-inspired North Korean army. Many people believed that the Soviet Union was in effect doing the shooting through a North Korean puppet. Some jittery people feared that it was the beginning of World War III.

With the Soviet Union boycotting the Security Council and therefore unable to wield the veto, that body immediately met and accepted an American resolution declaring the North Korean invasion to be a breach of the peace. The resolution also called for an immediate cessation of the fighting and the withdrawal of the invading troops. Finally, it called upon members of the United Nations "to render every assistance" in bringing an end to the aggression.

In response to the UN resolution, President Truman ordered American air and naval forces to help South Korea resist the invasion. Then he ordered a substantial part of the U.S. Army troops stationed in Japan to go to South Korea and defend it. Eventually, sixteen other countries supplied armed forces, though the chief military burden was borne by the Americans. The military command, which operated under the flag of the United Nations, was headed by American general Douglas MacArthur.

The fighting in Korea was to drag on for over three years, at great cost in lives and money. Of the more than one million American who served, about 150,000 were wounded and 33,000 died. But in the end, the North Koreans were defeated in their effort to conquer South

Korea and retreated into their own territory. The aggressors, too, had suffered enormous battle losses and ended up with fifteen hundred square miles less territory than they had when they started. The truce that was concluded on July 27, 1953, remained in force in the mid-1980s. Even then, no peace treaty had been signed; the problem of divided Korea's political future still remained unsolved.

In resisting the North Korean aggression, the United Nations appeared to have met a major challenge with decisiveness and success. But it had been able to act only because the Soviet Union made a tactical blunder by absenting itself from the Security Council, thus losing its ability to use a blocking veto. The Soviets returned to the Council in August 1950, but they could not undo the UN sponsorship of military action to halt North Korean aggression.

UNITING FOR PEACE

With the return of the Soviet Union to the Security Council, that body quickly reverted to a state of veto-bound impotence. Recognizing this, the Western powers—with questionable legality—attempted to bypass the Council and strengthen the General Assembly in the area of peacekeeping. To accomplish this, the United States introduced the "Uniting for Peace" resolution, which passed in the Assembly on November 3, 1950, by an overwhelming majority. In essence, it provided that if the Security Council, because of lack of unanimity among its five permanent members, fails to act on an apparent threat to the peace, breach of the peace, or act of aggression, the Assembly itself may take up the matter within twenty-four hours in an emergency special session. The resolution further provided that the Assembly could recommend collective measures, including the use of force.

As mentioned, the Uniting for Peace resolution was

of dubious legality. Although it did no more than empower the Assembly to *recommend* a course of action to member states, it was an encroachment on the peace-keeping authority granted by the Charter to the Security Council. As such, it was a virtual amendment of the Charter. The Soviet Union and its allies refused to recognize the resolution's legality. Ironically enough, in later years, when the Assembly came to be dominated by the Third World and Soviet bloc, the United States and its Western allies came to regard the Uniting for Peace resolution as a dead letter.

THE TRIBULATIONS
OF TRYGVE LIE

Secretary General Trygve Lie's support for the UN course in Korea caused the Soviet Union to veto his renomination at the expiration of his term in 1951. The United States, however, argued that Lie had acted quite properly on behalf of a collective security action undertaken by the United Nations and declared that it would veto any other candidate. Threatened with a deadlock in the Security Council (which must recommend a candidate to the Assembly), the Assembly nevertheless voted that Lie be "continued in office" for another three years.

But the issue was far from resolved. The Soviet Union, which regarded the Assembly's action as an illegal encroachment on the powers of the Security Council, flatly refused to recognize Lie as the secretary general. Russian diplomats boycotted him officially and socially; they insulted him personally. "He is unobjective, two-faced," said one of them. "We will have no truck with him." This severely limited the Norwegian's effectiveness and, indeed, crippled his ability to function as secretary general. As if Soviet hostility were not enough, Lie also came under attack by the anti-Communist followers of Senator Joseph McCarthy in the United States. They complained loudly that the United Nations Secretariat, unwittingly or not, had hired large numbers of "disloyal American citizens." The charges proved baseless, but it did not prevent the McCarthyites from sniping at Trygve Lie. At the same time, many members of the Secretariat thought that the secretary general was not sufficiently vigorous in refuting the accusations of the witch hunters.

Caught in the midst of ostracism by the Soviet Union, harassment from the McCarthyites, and a loss of confidence in him by some members of the Secretariat, Lie stunned the UN community on November 10, 1952, by announcing his intention of stepping down before the expiration of his extended term. He felt obliged, Lie told the General Assembly, to make way for a secretary general who had the confidence of the major powers. "I am stepping aside now because I hope this may help the United Nations to save the peace and to serve better the cause of freedom and progress for all mankind."

A search for a successor began at once, but it soon bogged down, since East and West could not agree on a candidate. Not until March 31, 1953, did the major powers agree on an acceptable successor to Lie. It was someone little known to the world at large: Dag Hammarskjold, minister of state in the Swedish Foreign Ministry. The Council's nomination was approved by the General Assembly, and on April 10 Hammarskjold was formally installed as secretary general for a five-year term. He himself was flabbergasted, commenting later that "I was simply picked out of a hat." Indeed, the Swede had been selected because he was offensive to no one and in the expectation that he would be content to play a largely passive role. But Hammarskjold, a man of keen intellect and wide learning, was to prove a tremendous surprise.

HAMMARSKJOLD TAKES OVER

When Hammarskjold arrived in New York on April 9, he was greeted by Trygve Lie, who gloomily told him that he was assuming "the most impossible job on this earth." But the new secretary general's first years at the United Nations passed with relative smoothness. The death of Soviet dictator Joseph Stalin led to a slight amelioration of Moscow's policies and a new strategy of "peaceful co-existence" with the West. The competition between the Communist bloc and the Western world continued but the Soviet rhetoric was less strident. In this somewhat more relaxed atmosphere, both the Soviet Union and the United States seemed quite pleased with Hammarskjold's performance, and he made every effort to be nonpartisan in the conduct of his office.

In 1955, the beginning of a shift in the political balance of power at the United Nations occurred with the admission of sixteen additional countries to membership. Since its inception, membership in the world body had risen slowly from fifty-one to sixty, largely because East and West refused to admit the other side's candidates. But now a package deal was worked out, one based not on the merits of each country's application for membership but on political bargaining. Four of the sixteen new members, Albania, Bulgaria, Hungary, and Romania, were from the Communist bloc. Six—Austria, Eire, Finland, Italy, Portugal, and Spain—were Western European states. Jordan and Libya came from the Arab world, while Cambodia, Ceylon (now Sri Lanka), Laos, and Nepal were Asian.

This was the beginning of the end of American and Western European domination of the United Nations. The four Communist-bloc countries, of course, were solidly anti-Western votes. The six Western European nations were a mixed lot, each with its own special interest, hardly a dependable bloc of votes. From the standpoint of UN voting patterns, the six new Arab and Asian members were the most interesting. None was blatantly unfriendly toward the West, but all were former colonies of Western powers and some retained a degree of antagonism toward their former masters and toward colonialism in general. The world body was entering a period of flux, in which the East-West conflict was to become complicated by the appearance on the scene of new nations with their own interests, ambitions, and equal voting rights in the General Assembly. New challenges and new opportunities lay ahead for the United Nations and Dag Hammarskjold.

Not until 1956 did Hammarskjold have to face crises involving the major powers, and then he had to face two at once: one in the Suez Canal, the other in Hungary.

THE SUEZ CRISIS

The Suez crisis erupted as the result of the nationalization of the Suez Canal by Egyptian President Gamal Abdel Nasser in 1956. Until then the canal was owned by private foreign stockholders, chiefly French and British. Legally, Egypt was perfectly within its rights to take over the canal, providing it paid proper compensation to the stockholders and kept the international waterway open to all shippers. But the governments of France and Britain, disturbed by Nasser's precipitous action and determined to establish international control over the canal, decided to seize it by military force. In collusion with Israel, which had territorial designs on Egypt's Sinai Peninsula, they hatched a plan.

On October 29, Israel invaded the Sinai and quickly pushed to the edge of the Suez Canal. Two days later, while the United Nations was deploring the Israeli act, French and British aircraft bombarded Egyptian military targets and dropped tens of thousands of airborne troops into the Suez area. There was a minimum of resistance and the invaders quickly seized key points around the waterway.

In response, the UN General Assembly passed resolutions calling for a cease-fire and the withdrawal of the invading forces. The Soviet Union, then an ally of Egypt and its chief military supplier, made a series of bombastic threats to Britain, France, and Israel, but at the same time it angered Egypt by refusing its urgent requests for fresh military equipment. As it turned out, it was the United States that put an end to the crisis. An angry President Dwight D. Eisenhower, leader of the Western alliance, had been kept totally in the dark about the British-French-Israeli plan to attack Egypt. On November 5, Eisenhower demanded that the invading forces heed UN resolutions and withdraw from Egypt. The three countries could do little but comply with the wishes of their powerful ally and military protector. The British and French withdrew their troops by December 23, their mission to prevent the Egyptian takeover of the Suez Canal a dismal failure. The Israelis, who at first announced their intention to annex the Sinai, reluctantly pulled their forces out by March 1957.

In throwing its support behind the United Nations, the United States had done much to build the prestige of the organization. Moreover, Secretary General Hammarskjold emerged from the Suez crisis with an enhanced reputation for effectiveness. In response to a UN resolution, Hammarskjold quickly devised a plan for a United Nations Emergency Force to serve as a buffer between Egyptian troops and the invaders. So quickly did his staff operate that the first contingents of UN troops arrived in Egypt on November 15, 1956; by mid-December, five thousand troops, drawn from neutral countries, were deployed. UNEF, as it was called, thus became the first large United Nations peacekeeping force. It remained effectively in place until 1967 (see page 66).

UPRISING IN HUNGARY

The United Nations was far less successful in the case of Hungary. At the same time as the early stages of the hostilities in Egypt, popular demonstrations for greater freedom in Communist Hungary quickly flared into a widespread revolt against Russian domination of their country. Carried away by the heady wine of freedom, the Communist government in Budapest asserted its independence of Moscow and renounced the Warsaw military pact, which bound them to the Soviet Union. This was going too far for the Russian leaders. Unwilling to see one of their satellites leave the Soviet orbit, they sent thousands of tanks into the volatile Budapest area and brutally suppressed the uprising by slaughtering thousands of rebels in the streets.

Repeated resolutions in the General Assembly calling on the Soviets to withdraw their troops were simply ignored. Instead, they ejected the old Communist government, which had proved far too nationalistic for their taste, and installed a new one, which was totally subservient to Moscow. The Assembly condemned the Soviet Union for a "violation of the Charter," but it was nothing more than a slap on the wrist. Hungary remained under Soviet domination.

The conclusion to be drawn from the crisis in Hungary was that when one of the great powers chose to defy the United Nations, it could do so with impunity. The organization's inability to respond effectively once again demonstrated that its powers were severely limited and that compliance with its wishes are essentially voluntary in nature.

FOCUS ON AFRICA

As the 1960s approached, Secretary General Hammarskjold became increasingly convinced that the United Nations would have a major role to play in Africa—and that Africa would have a major role to play in the United Nations. He was right on both counts. The rapid emancipation of colonial dependencies in the 1950s led to the addition of seventeen new members in 1960 alone, and all but one of them were from Africa. The admission of Nigeria raised the UN membership to 100. By 1963, the number of states in the United Nations reached 111, of which 58 were former colonial states from Asia or Africa. For the first time, the United States and its allies faced the prospect of being frequently outvoted in the General Assembly by the Afro-Asians and their supporters.

It was clear to Hammarskjold that the African states, in particular, would need the special help and guidance of the United Nations. Many of the new African countries were badly prepared for freedom by their former colonial masters. With boundaries artificially contrived by their previous European administrators, many of the African countries were driven by tribal antagonisms and shackled with unstable political structures. More than previous entrants into the ranks of the United Nations, they had to lean heavily on the organization for aid of all kinds. Hammarskjold was fully aware of the fragile nature of some of the new African republics and thus was not surprised when the Congo crisis burst upon the world in the summer of 1960.

THE CONGO IN CONVULSION

On June 30, 1960, the colony known as the Belgian Congo, a vast territory in the heart of Africa, gained its independence. The Belgian colonial administrators had done little to prepare the country for freedom. It had few trained civil servants, practically no technicians, only a handful of college graduates, and not many responsible political leaders. Almost immediately after independence, Congolese troops mutinied against their white Belgian officers, who had been left behind to help train the army. As the world looked on in horror, the rebellious soldiers subjected the Europeans in the country to an orgy of looting, rape, and murder. The Belgians reacted by halting the withdrawal of their troops and rushing reinforcements into the Congo to restore order. At that point, Patrice Lumumba, the erratic first Congolese premier, appealed to the United Nations for help against Belgian "aggression."

Lumumba, who had pro-Soviet sympathies, made it clear that unless the United Nations took action he would ask the Soviet Union to send in troops to expel the Belgians. The situation was highly explosive. Taking its cue from Lumumba, the Soviet Union threatened to intervene in the name of anticolonialism. The Belgians and other Western countries had valuable economic interests in the Congo, particularly in the mineral-rich province of Katanga, and they were anxious to preserve them. Meanwhile, the newly independent country seemed ready to lapse back into anarchy.

From the outset, Hammarskjold took the lead. It was the secretary general, not any member state, who requested an emergency meeting of the Security Council, which passed a resolution asking the Belgians to withdraw. The Council also gave Hammarskjold a loosely worded mandate to "provide . . . such military assistance as may be necessary" to restore order in the Congo. Hammarskjold then recommended the creation of a UN force that came to be known as ONUC (from its French title, *Organisation des Nations Unies au Congo*) and proposed that it be composed chiefly of troops from African states. When the Council accepted these views, the secretary general moved with his customary dispatch. By July 17, about thirty-five hundred troops from Tunisia, Ghana, Morocco, and Ethiopia arrived in the Congo under the UN flag. Contingents of Swedes and Indians followed soon thereafter. Order was quickly restored in the capital (then called Leopoldville), if not in the countryside, and as the UN forces multiplied they took over from the Belgians. In August, the Belgian armed forces were able to withdraw totally from the Congo.

ONUC, whose numbers would rise to twenty thousand within months, faced a truly formidable task—control of a chaotic country four times the size of France.

Secretary General Dag Hammarskjold (second from left)
at the Leopoldville airfield in the Congo in 1961.
Five days later he was killed in a plane crash while
on his way to meet with the leader
of the Katanga secessionist movement.

Moreover, in addition to ONUC's military mission, Hammarskjold's UN Secretariat had to conduct an extensive civilian operation. All the UN's specialized agencies were mobilized to restore and maintain essential services, supervise food distribution, advise on finances, revamp the judiciary and legal system, train government workers, and establish a public works program. As Hammarskjold said, "the Congo crisis . . . put the Secretariat under the heaviest strain which it has ever had to face." Some critics charged that the UN and the secretary general in particular were taking on too much authority, but defenders pointed out that the alternatives were anarchy or intervention by the major powers.

THE KATANGA SECESSION

Adding to the complexity of the UN's task was the problem of Katanga, the economically strong province which attempted to secede from the Congo in July 1960. This move, initiated by Katanga's President Moise Tshombe and supported by Belgian and other foreign financial interests, threatened the stability of the Congo itself and all of central Africa. If the Katanga secession succeeded, other separatist movements throughout Africa would have taken heart. At first Hammarskjold refrained from using UN troops to put down the secession, fearing that he did not have the authority to do so. For this reticence, the secretary general earned the outspoken displeasure of Lumumba and his Soviet supporters.

The Soviet Union had other reasons for taking an increasingly harsh view of Hammarskjold. The Russians had always been opposed to a strong secretary general, one who would become a political force in his own right and a leader of world opinion. Hammarskjold suited Moscow as long as he remained a low-key figure in the background. But now, in the Congo, he was in charge of a massive operation, directing a large military force and an unprecedented civilian effort, making day-to-day decisions that inevitably had a political impact. Moreover, although Moscow had initially supported the UN operation in the Congo in hopes that it would prop up Patrice Lumumba, it now saw that things were not working out as expected. In August and September 1960, a fierce political struggle, exacerbated by tribal rivalries, broke out in the Congo, and in the end Lumumba was ousted from office and arrested by pro-Western Congolese. A short time later, the fiery leader was transferred to a prison in Katanga, whose secessionist leader Tshombe was then being wooed by the new leaders in Leopoldville in hopes that he would end his attempt to establish a separate state. Soon after his arrival in Katanga, Patrice Lumumba disappeared and was thought to have been murdered by the Katangan military.

By now the Soviet Union was furious, accusing the United Nations of connivance in Lumumba's death. Soviet delegates to the world body demanded the discontinuance of the Congo operation and Hammarskjold's dismissal as secretary general. "We do not, and cannot, place confidence in Mr. Hammarskjold," declared a Soviet spokesman. "If he cannot muster the courage to resign in, let us say, a chivalrous way, we shall draw the inevitable conclusions from the situation." Despite the Soviet attitude, the General Assembly, including a great majority of the African members, gave the secretary general a ringing endorsement: it even voted him the authority to use force, if necessary, to resolve the threat posed by Katanga's secession.

It was a heartening vote of confidence in Hammarskjold. At first the secretary general did all he could to persuade Tshombe to end the secession and join in an all-Congolese government; but the Katangan—encouraged by foreign business interests and emboldened by the European mercenary soldiers who commanded his army—refused to back down. Hammarskjold thereupon ordered the UN army into action. After initial actions ended in many casualties for the UN forces, the secretary general agreed to talks on a cease-fire. He then decided to conduct the talks without intermediaries. On the night of September 17–18, 1961, en route to a meeting with Tshombe, his plane crashed outside the airport at Ndola, Northern Rhodesia. Hammarskjold and all the other occupants were killed.

On September 19, Frederick Boland of Ireland opened the annual session of the General Assembly "in the shadow of an immense tragedy." In his masterful book, *Hammarskjold*, Brian Urquhart described the scene: "At the United Nations, shock, grief and a pervading sense of acute personal loss were mingled with general dismay. Though Hammarskjold had been criticized from all sides in the past year, his empty chair on the podium of the General Assembly Hall symbolized the void left in the life of the Organization by the sudden and permanent absence of his active leadership."

Had Hammarskjold not been killed in the active service of the United Nations, he almost certainly would have suffered the same fate as his predecessor, Trygve Lie. The Soviet Union, totally alarmed by his activism in extending the authority of the secretary general, had begun to ignore Hammarskjold and revile him. His position would have been impossible. The sad truth is that no secretary general can function for long if one of the two superpowers, the Soviet Union or the United States, has decided that he is acting against its vital interests.

THIRD WORLD
ASCENDANCY

The crisis caused by Hammarskjold's death even over-shadowed the Congo question for a time. For over six weeks the Soviet Union held out against the appointment of any successor to fill Hammarskjold's unexpired term. Moscow did not want another activist secretary general; in fact, it did not want a secretary general at all. Instead, Soviet spokesmen advanced a scheme called a "troika." Named for a three-horse Russian sleigh, the troika would have replaced the secretary general with a three-man directorate representing various voting blocs. In short, the troika would have been an absolute guarantee of ineffectiveness at the top of the Secretariat.

The Western nations opposed the Soviet proposal strenuously, and in the end the Third World countries—chiefly the Africans, Asians, and Latin Americans—came to see it as an attack on the UN system they had found so congenial. Finally, the Russians had to give way. On November 3, 1961, Burma's U Thant, a highly regarded, low-key diplomat who had offended no one, was unanimously selected as acting secretary general to fill out the remainder of Hammarskjold's term. U Thant, whose name translated into English as "Mr. Clean," was later elected to two full five-year terms. His selection was, among other things, a direct reflection of the growing influence of the Third World at the United Nations.

HIGH-WATER MARK

Upon assuming office, U Thant first had to come to grips with the lingering Congo crisis. A cease-fire negotiated with Tshombe quickly fell apart, and as a result the Security Council authorized the secretary general to use force to complete the removal of the European mercenaries from Katanga. His authority strengthened, U Thant ordered UN troops into action to "re-establish law and order and to protect life and property" as well as to secure "complete freedom of movement" for the UN forces in Katanga.

On December 5, UN forces, complete with tanks and aircraft, struck hard at Tshombe's military positions. Many people in the United States and elsewhere were shocked to see a UN army actually waging war and not merely interposing itself between two opposing sides. But the Kennedy administration, anxious to bring stability to the Congo, vigorously supported U Thant's efforts to corral Katanga.

By late December, Tshombe agreed to a new cease-fire and to negotiate with Cyrille Adoula, the Congolese premier, on an end to the secession. But Tshombe still had his European mercenaries, and it was soon evident that he was in no hurry to reach an agreement with Adoula. In August 1962, U Thant proposed a "plan of national reconstruction," which provided for a federal constitution and a central administration that would offer representation to all tribal and provincial groups. When Tshombe continued to stall, U Thant once again sent UN troops into action. This time the action, carried out largely by crack Indian units, was decisive. Resistance collapsed, and on January 15, 1963, Tshombe announced the end of Katanga's secession, dismissed the mercenaries, and accepted U Thant's plan for the reconstruction of the Congo.

Due to widespread violence in many parts of the Congo, ONUC remained in being until a national army could be trained. The UN force was finally withdrawn and disbanded in June 1964, leaving behind a reasonably stable, reunified country where only disorder and mayhem had existed before it came.

In the aftermath of the Congo operation, the organization's role as a peacekeeper was to be kept strictly in check. Not only the Soviet Union, but later the Western powers, looked askance at the usurpation by the General Assembly of the Security Council's Charter-given authority as the keeper of peace and security. Moreover, the Soviet Union remained adamantly opposed to any extension of the powers of the secretary general. U Thant, a cautious man, understood this perfectly well; in order to hold the organization together he would have to show a low profile when the interests of the major powers were concerned.

THE MISSILE CRISIS

U Thant's cautious but constructive approach to questions involving conflict between the superpowers was evident during the Cuban missile crisis of 1962, the hottest hour of the Cold War. In October of that year, the United States discovered through aerial reconnaissance that the Soviet Union was placing nuclear missiles in Cuba that would be able to threaten population centers in North and South America. In response, President Kennedy did not turn to the United Nations, where debate might have been inconclusive, but clamped a "quarantine" on all ships carrying offensive weapons to Communist Cuba. This meant that if Soviet ships headed for Cuba failed to stop and submit to a search,

U.S. ships were authorized to fire on them. If that had happened, it might have meant war between the United States and the Soviet Union.

As the world trembled on the brink of nuclear war, President Kennedy and Soviet leader Nikita Khrushchev engaged in urgent exchanges of messages. Convinced of the determination of the American president and of the danger of an all-out war, Khrushchev backed away from a collision course and recalled a number of ships bound for Cuba with nuclear weapons. A thoroughly rattled Khrushchev also agreed to withdraw the nuclear missiles already installed in Cuba in exchange for a pledge by Kennedy that the United States would not invade Cuba. The deal was made and the missiles were withdrawn.

In the most dangerous confrontation between the superpowers since the invention of the atom bomb, the crisis was solved by Kennedy and Khrushchev, not by the United Nations. True, U Thant and his staff were active behind the scenes, smoothing out details once the major decisions were made by the superpowers, but the fact was that while the world faced catastrophe, the United Nations was largely bypassed. Moreover, when U Thant tried to persuade Cuban leader Fidel Castro to allow the United Nations to supervise the dismantling of the rocket sites, he met with a blunt refusal. The missile crisis demonstrated once again that in a confrontation between the United States and the Soviet Union the role of the United Nations, and the secretary general, is necessarily a marginal one.

REMOVAL OF UNEF

A good example of U Thant's cautious approach in the use of his office came in 1967, when the eleven-year truce between Israel and its Arab neighbors was broken by Arab raids and Israeli retaliatory air strikes. As the tension mounted, Egyptian president Gamal Abdel Nasser apparently felt that it was time to test his Soviet-equipped army and air force against the Israelis. Accordingly, he demanded that the United Nations withdraw the United Nations Emergency Force, whose troops had been positioned between the Egyptians and Israelis since the end of the Suez crisis.

U Thant was in a ticklish position. Egypt clearly was within its rights in asking for UNEF's removal, since the original agreement between Hammarskjold and Nasser provided that the UN force would enter Egyptian territory only with Egypt's consent. (There were no UNEF troops on the Israeli side of the border, since Israel had refused to have them stationed there.) But removal of the UNEF soldiers would almost certainly increase the chances of another Arab-Israeli war. In such a situation, Dag Hammarskjold might have found a way to postpone decisions, to consult advisers, to mobilize the opinion of influential members of the United Nations, to meet with Nasser and try to talk him out of his course of action. But U Thant, aware that the Soviet Union and other powers preferred a secretary general who did not intrude too forcibly in crises involving the great powers or their allies, played it strictly by the book. He agreed—all too quickly, critics said—to Nasser's request to withdraw UNEF.

With the UN force gone, Nasser, on May 22, 1967, closed shipping to Israel in the narrow Gulf of Aqaba, a shipping channel that provided access to Israel's only southern port. At that point, the Israelis, convinced that the Egyptians and their Arab allies were planning to strike, decided to move first. On June 5, Israel unleashed a devastating air and ground attack on Egypt, Syria, and Jordan which in six days completely routed the Arab states. As a result, Israel occupied large chunks of Arab territory—the West Bank of the Jordan, the Golan Heights of Syria, and the Sinai Peninsula of Egypt. It should be noted that the Security Council passed a number of resolutions calling for a cease-fire while the battle was raging. The resolutions were ignored—until the Israelis had achieved their objectives.

SOME LOW POINTS

The latter part of the 1960s was not a golden age for the United Nations. In Vietnam, an extraordinarily destructive and seemingly endless war raged as the world body looked on with total impotence. Neither of the local rivals, North Vietnam and South Vietnam, was a member of the United Nations; each half of the country claimed to represent the whole. Hundreds of thousands of words were uttered in the General Assembly, denouncing one side or the other, but the United States, heavily involved in supporting South Vietnam with money, equipment, and fighting men, refused to allow the United Nations a significant role. The American extrication from the Vietnam quagmire was engineered by the United States and North Vietnam. The war was to end through North Vietnamese military victory and not through diplomacy.

Another example of UN impotence came in Czechoslovakia. In 1968, when that Eastern European country's Communist government attempted to liberalize its policies and loosen its ties with Moscow, Russian tanks rumbled into the Czechoslovakian capital of Prague, arrested the government leaders, and replaced them with more reliable Soviet puppets. It was Hungary all over again. A Security Council resolution condemning the "armed intervention" and calling for an immediate Soviet withdrawal was blocked by a Soviet veto. Once again the hands of the United Nations were tied.

The feebleness of the world body as a peacekeeper was demonstrated once again in December 1971, when war broke out between India and Pakistan. The fighting developed when Pakistan attempted to put down an insurgency in its eastern segment and India intervened on the side of the rebels. Once India and Pakistan became involved in full-scale warfare, the Security Council addressed the issue with all too predictable results. Time after time, the Soviet Union, an ally of India, vetoed resolutions sponsored by the United States that called for an immediate cease-fire and the withdrawal of Indian and Pakistani forces behind their own borders. With the war going badly for Pakistan, its foreign minister, Zulfikar Ali Bhutto, addressed the deadlocked Council and accused it of "legalizing aggression." Not until the Indian army achieved its military objectives, enabling the insurgents to carve a new country named Bangladesh out of Pakistan, did the Council pass a resolution calling for a cease-fire and withdrawal of forces. It was another low point for the United Nations.

THE CHINA QUESTION

The year 1971 was also to see the long-simmering debate over the admission of the Communist Chinese government in Beijing (Peking) reach a climax in the General Assembly. For years the United States had fought successfully to retain China's seat in the United Nations for the Nationalist Chinese government, which was based on Taiwan. But now the votes in the Assembly, where matters of seating credentials are settled, were on the side of Beijing's entry. Fighting a rear-guard battle, the United States held out for a "two-China" solution—UN membership for both the Beijing and Taiwan governments. This U.S. plan was defeated in October 1971, and the Communist government in Beijing became the sole occupant of China's seat in the United Nations. Whatever one might have thought of the Beijing government, it was undeniable that the recognition of a regime that ruled almost a quarter of the world's population was a belated victory for realism.

The admission of the Beijing government into membership in the United Nations had a decided impact on the world body. It was not that the revolutionary new member proceeded to sabotage the operations of the organization. Instead of creating havoc, the new group of Chinese diplomats settled in peacefully, behaving with the utmost civility and correctness. But their presence did introduce a new complexity into UN affairs. Where previously the United Nations had been a political battleground between two rival systems—roughly the Western democracies and their allies versus the Soviet bloc of Communist states and their allies—now an important new factor had to be considered. China was a major country governed by a Marxist-Leninist (or Communist) government that was profoundly at odds with the Soviet Union and its Communist bloc. Moreover, as a "lesser-developed country" (an LDC, as they are sometimes called at the United Nations), China had a good deal in common with many of the Third World nations. As a result, the delegates from Beijing quickly adopted a two-pronged UN strategy of wooing the Third World nations and baiting the Soviet Union. Previously bored UN observers watched with delight as the two leading Communist powers of the world, China and the Soviet Union, exchanged the most venomous of insults across the horseshoe-shaped table of the Security Council.

Although the entry of the Communist Chinese was at first perceived to be a major diplomatic defeat for the United States, the Nixon administration was quick to recognize the new realities. Just three months after the United Nations admitted Communist China, Richard Nixon became the first American president to visit Beijing and open the door to vastly improved relations between the United States and China.

WALDHEIM SUCCEEDS
U THANT

At the end of 1971, U Thant's second full term came to an end, and in view of his poor health, the Burmese discouraged efforts to draft him for another term. After days of diplomatic maneuvering, the Security Council unanimously agreed upon Kurt Waldheim to succeed U Thant, a choice that was unanimously accepted by the Assembly. Waldheim came from Austria, a "neutral" country. He had experience at the United Nations, where he had been head of Austria's mission, and in world affairs generally, as previous foreign minister of his country. And he was uncontroversial. Tall, thin, impeccably dressed in dark suits, Waldheim was soon dubbed by UN correspondents "the head waiter."

Waldheim was fortunate that his first years in office coincided with the development of *détente,* or relaxation of tensions between East and West. Debate was less strident, and the improved atmosphere led to a solution to the long-standing "two Germanies" problem. With both sides in accord, democratic West Germany and Communist East Germany were admitted to membership on the same day, September 18, 1973.

In October 1973 the diplomatic calm ended when the smoldering Arab-Israeli dispute burst into flames again. This time Egypt and Syria struck first, and for a time it looked as if Israel might be defeated. But with the aid of a massive American airlift of tanks, planes, and other military equipment, the Israelis were able to rally and take the offensive. But then a superpower confrontation became a distinct possibility when the Soviet Union threatened to intervene on the side of the Arabs and President Nixon ordered American military forces to go on a "precautionary alert."

The crisis eased only after urgent messages were exchanged between Washington and Moscow, and after Secretary of State Henry Kissinger hastily flew to Moscow to confer with Soviet leader Leonid Brezhnev. The two sides found enough common ground to enable the Security Council to agree on a resolution calling for a cease-fire, negotiations, and the re-establishment of the United Nations Emergency Force that U Thant had dis-

UN observers in Syria's
Golan Heights in 1973

banded in 1967. The new UNEF, over five thousand strong, was quickly dispatched to the Middle East and took positions between the Egyptian and Israeli armies, thus permitting both to disengage. A smaller force, the United Nations Disengagement Observer Force (UN-DOF), was sent to the Israeli-Syrian front and separated the warring armies in that area. Once again, the role of the United Nations in restoring peace to the Middle East proved to be limited—but indispensable.

If the United Nations had again demonstrated its utility as a peacekeeper in the Middle East, its image suffered in the tortured land of Cyprus. Since its formation in 1964, the United Nations Force in Cyprus (UNFI-CYP) had successfully kept the peace between the Greek majority (82 percent) and the Turkish minority (18 percent) on the island republic in the Mediterranean. But in July 1974 troops from mainland Turkey descended on Cyprus, swept aside the UN force, and effectively partitioned the island into Turkish and Greek zones. While all this was going on, the Turkish government failed to heed the unanimous resolutions of the Security Council until its call for a cease-fire had been made four times. During the fighting, thirty-six members of UNFICYP were killed. Once the fighting was over, all sides turned to UNFICYP to help police the cease-fire agreement. Still, it was a blow to the prestige of the United Nations and yet another reminder of its limited power in a world of conflicting national interests and warring ideologies.

THE POWER OF
THE THIRD WORLD

A trend that began in the 1950s and accelerated during the 1960s, the growing influence at the United Nations of the smaller, weaker nations, became a factor of major importance in the mid-1970s. As was to be expected, the interests of many Third World countries, a number of them recently emerged from colonial status, did not always coincide with those of the United States and its allies. Since these developing countries now commanded a substantial majority in the General Assembly, where each member has one vote without regard to the country's size or power, they were able to push through many resolutions deemed unnecessarily provocative by the Western world. Sometimes they would vote to pass contradictory resolutions on the same day, and to the dismay of those countries that footed the bills, the Third World nations often voted to increase the organization's budget to finance pet projects or to swell the Secretariat's bureaucracy with new commissions or committees.

Little wonder that some Western observers came to question the performance of the General Assembly. In 1974, U.S. ambassador John Scali and other diplomats openly spoke out against the "tryanny of the majority" formed by the developing countries. Third World spokesmen, however, pointed out that the United States and its allies did not complain about the General Assembly when they had dominated it in the earlier years of that body. And Secretary General Waldheim, at the close of the Assembly session in 1974, remarked that it had been "one of the most important sessions in the history of the United Nations" because it "reflected and recorded the political tides and changes of our world and the new forces in world affairs." This trend, added Waldheim, "cannot be an entirely comfortable process."

THE MIDDLE EAST

On the subject of Israel, for example, the Third World majority was relentless in its attack—sometimes to the point of being farcical. In 1974, it invited Yasir Arafat, then the unchallenged leader of the Palestine Liberation Organization (PLO) and commander of its guerrilla war against Israel, to address the General Assembly. It was an unprecedented insult to a member state, Israel. Arafat, who was awarded all the honors usually reserved for rep-

(73)

resentatives of member states, delivered a militant speech and was rewarded by a standing ovation from the delegates. The same session of the Assembly then voted to grant the PLO observer status at the United Nations, thus allowing it to use UN facilities at will. Said one bitter Israeli diplomat: "That would be like inviting the Irish Republican Army to send a spokesman to address the Assembly and be given observer status. Really incredible, giving diplomatic status to pure terrorists."

Needless to say, the Third World majority in the Assembly did not agree with that assessment. Many of them, especially the Africans and Asians who had recently fought for their countries' independence, identified with the Palestinians and with the PLO's widely perceived objective: an independent state for the Palestinian people. Others among the Third World states were so dependent on oil from Arab countries that they did not dare to vote differently than the Arab members in the Assembly. Still others were playing a routine game of trade-off with the Arab countries: You support us on our issues, say those of southern Africa, and we support you when it comes to Israel. This complexity of motives led the Assembly majority to take its anti-Israel campaign an abrasive step further in 1975. In one of the most turbulent sessions ever held by the General Assembly, a large majority voted to brand Zionism, the Jewish nationalist movement that had led to the formation of Israel, a "form of racism."

The extreme anti-Israel tone of this resolution horrified many supporters of Israel. But it also had a numbing effect on public opinion. In the years that followed, the Assembly sometimes had sound reasons for criticizing Israel: its treatment of Arabs in areas occupied by Israel, its annexation of the old city of Jerusalem, its annexation of Syria's Golan Heights, and its establishment of permanent settlements on the West Bank of the Jordan, to name only a few. But by the late 1970s the Assembly had passed so many resolutions critical of Israel that the world paid little attention.

The growing irrelevance of the United Nations to major diplomacy in the Middle East was forcefully demonstrated in 1978 when President Jimmy Carter played host to Israeli prime minister Menachem Begin and Egyptian president Anwar Sadat at Camp David, Maryland. From this meeting emerged the outlines of the Israel-Egypt peace treaty, which was signed in Washington a year later. The historic, first treaty between Israel and an Arab state led to diplomatic ties between the two states, the withdrawal by Israel from the Sinai Peninsula, and the very real possibility that Egypt and Israel would not again contend on the battlefield. Although Secretary General Waldheim was kept informed by Washington about progress in the negotiations, it was clear that this landmark in modern diplomacy was conducted entirely outside the world organization. Following the lead of most of the Arab states, the General Assembly voted overwhelmingly to protest the tripartite diplomacy of the United States, Israel, and Egypt.

But if the United Nations was outside the mainstream of Middle East diplomacy, the world body continued to serve limited practical purposes. In 1978, after Israel responded to PLO attacks with a massive invasion of southern Lebanon, the Security Council established a new UN peacekeeping operation called the United Nations Interim Force in Lebanon (UNIFIL). Once the Israelis achieved their stated objective of smashing PLO guerrilla bases and withdrew, UNIFIL moved into southern Lebanon. But the effectiveness of the UN force in providing stability in that area was limited by the withdrawing Israelis. Instead of permitting UNIFIL to move into critical regions north of the Israeli border, the Israelis—who questioned the UN's ability to prevent guerrilla infiltration—turned over control to pro-Israel, Christian militiamen.

In 1978 Secretary General Kurt Waldheim met with Israel's Foreign Minister Moshe Dayan to discuss UN resolutions calling for Israeli withdrawal from Lebanese territory, and provisions for the UN Interim Force in Lebanon.

SOUTHERN AFRICA

In the years of Kurt Waldheim's secretary generalship (1972–1981), the African countries became the single largest voting bloc in the United Nations. As a consequence, African affairs came to the forefront of attention at the world body. In the areas of economic, technical, educational, and medical assistance, the United Nations and its various agencies became extremely active throughout most of Africa. But when it came to diplomatic influence, the United Nations was not an important factor, since the highly partisan positions expressed in the General Assembly and Security Council disqualified it from objective mediatory roles. This was particularly true in southern Africa, where black liberation groups struggled for independence or political equality against white-ruled governments and racial battlelines were being drawn.

Rhodesia, a prosperous white-ruled country on the northern border of South Africa, was a good example. Throughout the 1970s, UN bodies passed dozens of resolutions condemning the regime in Rhodesia, but the huffing and puffing accomplished very little. The actual transformation of white-ruled Rhodesia into black-ruled Zimbabwe was brought about by two things: the efforts of guerrilla fighters who sapped the strength of the government military forces, and the pressures exerted by Western powers, principally Britain and the United States, on behalf of democratic one-man-one-vote elections. Step by step, under the combined military and diplomatic pressures, the Rhodesian government agreed to have elections supervised by British troops. The elections took place in 1980, whereupon the black and white voters chose a black government for the independent state of Zimbabwe.

Throughout the Waldheim years, the white-supremacist government of South Africa remained a major target of the Third World nations in the UN. In 1974, the General Assembly condemned South Africa's racial policy of *apartheid* ("apartness" or segregation) and barred the country's delegation from participating in its deliberations. The same year, the Security Council was on the verge of stripping South Africa of its membership in the United Nations, only to be prevented by an historic first: three Western vetoes on the same day, cast by the United States, Britain, and France. These Western countries agreed, of course, that South Africa's official system of discrimination according to race, one that deprived the black majority of civil rights, was thoroughly deplorable. But they saw no value whatsoever in driving South Africa out of the world body, especially since the United Nations was committed to the principle of "universality," or membership for all member nations no matter how abhorrent their governments' policies might be.

In 1976, the General Assembly took the unprecedented step of endorsing "armed struggle" to overthrow the government of South Africa. After that, in resolution after resolution, year after year, the Assembly passionately condemned South Africa and demanded changes in its racial policies. The trouble was that all these resolutions lacked teeth, since the Assembly can only recommend actions to UN members, not require it. In 1977, however, the Security Council voted for a mandatory embargo on the sale of arms to South Africa by all members of the United Nations. This was the first and only time that the Council has voted a prohibition on arms sales to a member state that would be compulsory for other members. But even the Council's arms embargo was not very effective, since South Africa manufactures much of its own military equipment and easily finds dealers around the world who are ready to supply the remainder of its needs.

The UN role in South West Africa (Namibia) also demonstrated the virtues and weaknesses of the world body. But first, let us sketch in a little historical background. After World War I, the newly formed League of

Nations awarded South Africa the mandate to administer the vast territory of South West Africa, formerly a colony of defeated Germany. South Africa was obliged by the League to promote "to the utmost the material and moral well-being" of the territory's people. South Africa was not, in any sense, given sovereignty over the territory and its overwhelmingly black population.

In the years after World War II, South Africa wanted to annex the mineral-rich land outright, but the United Nations (as legal successor to the League) denied the request and placed South West Africa under trusteeship status. In other words, South Africa would continue to administer the territory, but it would have to account for its actions there to the United Nations. The International Court of Justice supported the United Nations in this position. But South Africa ignored these actions and attempted to graft its own system of racial *apartheid* onto South West Africa, provoking the General Assembly and the Security Council to declare South Africa's occupation of the territory to be illegal. The UN bodies also adopted a new, African name for the disputed land: Namibia.

During the Assembly session of 1976, a resolution was passed that called for "free elections [in Namibia] under the supervision and control of the United Nations." At the same time, the Assembly also recognized the South West Africa People's Organization (SWAPO), a left-wing guerrilla group with a wide following in Namibia, as the only legitimate claimant to power in the country. The General Assembly's open support of SWAPO, and its open dismissal of other political forces in the country, gave the South African government the opportunity to charge that the United Nations was biased and therefore not to be trusted in the supervision of free elections and the transition to independence in Namibia.

As a result, although the United Nations had championed the cause of an independent Namibia, its diplomatic role became increasingly peripheral. The South African government refused to discuss Namibia with the United Nations. In April 1977, five Western members of the Security Council (Britain, Canada, France, the United States, and West Germany) decided to do what the United Nations could not accomplish—open a dialogue with South Africa in an attempt to negotiate the independence of Namibia. The talks initiated by this so-called "contact group" of Western countries made considerable progress in the late 1970s. The contact group proposed a plan for a cease-fire between the South African army and SWAPO's guerrilla fighters, a phased withdrawal of South African troops over a seven-month period, the abolition of race laws, and the election of an assembly to draw up a constitution for an independent Namibia. SWAPO, which believed it would win a fair election in Namibia, accepted the plan; the government of South Africa, though far from enthusiastic, bowed to Western pressure and accepted the general outlines of the proposal.

In 1978, the Security Council incorporated the plan into a resolution that envisioned a United Nations Transition Assistance Group (UNTAG), composed of seventy-five hundred troops and fifteen hundred civilians to supervise the Namibian elections. But South Africa's doubts about the impartiality of such a UN supervisory force, in light of the General Assembly's stated support for SWAPO, remained an obstacle to a settlement. Time after time, South Africa backed away from a final agreement, believing that SWAPO was an ally of the Soviet Union and that a SWAPO-led government in Namibia would amount to having a Soviet colony on its northern border.

Should Namibia gain independence, the United Nations will be able to claim considerable credit for keeping the issue alive over the years. It upheld the principle of self-determination and created a worldwide constituency for the independence of Namibia. On the other hand, it jeopardized its role as honest broker, giving South Africa the opportunity to raise one roadblock after the other to the practical plans advanced by the Western contact group.

If the rise of the Third World, the explosive realities of the Middle East, and a sharpening focus on southern Africa were salient features of Kurt Waldheim's tenure as secretary general, other major events—some of them deeply shocking—also engaged the attention of the world body in the late 1970s.

SOUTHEAST ASIA

In the aftermath of the Communist military victory in Southeast Asia in 1975, Cambodia was plunged into a state of misery and terror. For over three years, a small group of fanatics who ruled in the capital of Phnom Penh made a determined effort to "purify" the country of Western, urban, or non-Communist intellectual influences. The campaign took the lives of from one to three million Cambodians, through execution, brutality, and deprivation, often under the most horrible of circumstances. When word of this holocaust began to leak out, Western nations raised the issue at the United Nations, but their efforts received little support. China, an ally of Cambodia at the time, made the legally correct argument that the internal affairs of a member state were no business of the United Nations. As the Cambodians writhed in what Secretary General Waldheim called "a tragedy perhaps unparalleled in history," the United Nations looked on, helpless.

The bloodbath ended in January 1979, when Vietnamese troops invaded Cambodia, seized most of the country, and installed a new government. The Vietnamese, who were also Communist-ruled, launched the invasion for a number of reasons, none of them humanitarian. For decades, the Vietnamese Communists had regarded themselves as leaders of the Communist move-

(81)

ment in all of Indochina, including Laos and Cambodia as well as Vietnam itself. When the Cambodians refused to recognize their primacy, the Vietnamese decided to bring them to heel. Another major reason for the invasion was the fierce struggle between the Soviet Union and China for dominance within the Communist world. The Cambodians were pro-Chinese; the Vietnamese, firmly in the Soviet camp, were determined to eradicate Chinese influence in the region.

At the United Nations, the Security Council debated the Vietnamese invasion of Cambodia, but it could not pass a resolution because of Soviet vetoes cast on Vietnam's behalf. The General Assembly strongly supported a resolution calling for the withdrawal of all "foreign" (that is, Vietnamese) troops from Cambodia. But the Assembly's action was simply ignored by the Vietnamese government.

Meanwhile, world attention was aroused by the suffering of the people of Indochina. Fleeing the miseries of their homeland, hundreds of thousands of Cambodians piled into makeshift camps inside the Thailand border. More than a million Vietnamese also fled the repressive rule in their own country, often braving perilous seas in leaky boats in order to find refuge in Thailand, Malaysia, Taiwan, or Hongkong. As in other parts of the world with large numbers of refugees, the office of the UN High Commissioner for Refugees played a vital role in helping host countries cope with the problem of feeding, housing, and providing medical care for those who fled Indochina. Though sometimes hampered by the Vietnamese occupation force, UNICEF managed to deliver large amounts of food and medicine to the desperate people of Cambodia.

THE HOSTAGE CRISIS

In mid-March of 1979, shortly after the fundamentalist Muslim followers of the Ayatollah Ruhollah Khomeini seized power in Iran, Secretary General Waldheim appealed to the new rulers to halt the summary execution of opponents and critics of the regime. Waldheim's appeal was rudely rebuffed, a harbinger of things soon to come. In November, supporters of the Khomeini government seized the U.S. embassy in Teheran and took fifty-two American diplomats and marine guards hostage. When the Iranian government failed to secure their release and indeed encouraged the hostage-takers, Americans—and many millions of people around the world— were outraged by the undiplomatic behavior. Waldheim's repeated offers of his good offices to help resolve the crisis were brushed aside by the Iranians. The International Court of Justice and the Security Council, in a rare display of unanimity, called for the immediate release of the illegally held hostages. Every UN action was rejected by the Iranian government.

Finally, in January 1981, the Americans were released after 444 days of captivity under extremely harsh conditions. They were freed only after Algeria, acting as go-between, engineered a deal whereby the United States would release nearly $8 billion worth of Iranian assets that had been frozen in American bank accounts. In this crisis, the United Nations, and the secretary general in particular, had played an extremely active diplomatic role. But, as in many other instances, the only power the United Nations possessed was that of moral suasion. Faced with a government intent on violating the norms of international behavior, moral suasion clearly was not enough.

THE IRAN-IRAQ WAR

In the belief that Iran was weakened and disorganized by its revolutionary change of governments, Iraq unleashed a massive military attack on its neighbor in September 1980. Iraq hoped for a quick victory that would accomplish three things: contain the Khomeini revolution, whose followers also wished to topple the Iraqi government; seize control over the strategic Shatt al Arab waterway; and establish itself as the dominant power in the Persian Gulf area. During 1980 and most of 1981, Iraq gained control of sizable areas in southwestern Iran, but Iranian resistance stiffened and in the next few years the two sides engaged in a seesaw battle in which hundreds of thousands of people were killed and billions of dollars' worth of property destroyed.

A series of UN fact-finding missions and resolutions imploring both sides to observe a cease-fire and accept UN mediation failed to halt the fighting. Cease-fire appeals were consistently rejected by Iran and, on some occasions, by Iraq. Interest in UN mediation depended on which side was favored by the tide of battle at any given time, and so the killing went on.

THE SOVIETS IN AFGHANISTAN

In order to prop up a puppet Communist government in Afghanistan, a country situated in southern Asia between Iran and Pakistan, the Soviet Union invaded in late December 1979. By 1981, the Soviets had built their strength to a force of about 200,000 men. They and the troops of the pro-Soviet government in Kabul engaged in a fierce struggle with Muslim tribesmen, anti-Communist guerrillas, and army elements who defected to the rebel side. Despite a tremendous superiority in equipment and armament, the Soviet troops and their Afghan supporters were unable to put down the insurgents. Casualties ran high on both sides, and millions of refugees poured across the Afghan border into Iran and Pakistan.

Many members of the Third World opposed the Soviet Union on this issue. In 1980, the General Assembly voted overwhelmingly to condemn the invasion and outlined four requirements for ending the conflict: withdrawal of outside military forces; the right of self-determination; restoration of an independent, nonaligned Afghanistan; and provision for the voluntary return of the more than three million Afghan refugees in Pakistan and Iran. In 1981, Waldheim sent high-level representatives to Afghanistan and to Pakistan, the chief supporter of the rebels, to promote the General Assembly's plan. But the pro-Soviet government in Afghanistan, dependent on the Soviet troops for its survival, rejected it as unrealistic and one-sided. There was little that the United Nations could do. A major power, the Soviet Union, was deeply involved in the Afghanistan struggle, and it—much like the United States in Vietnam—was determined to keep the United Nations from playing a significant role.

WALDHEIM EXITS

The year 1981 marked the end of the Waldheim era at the United Nations. The Austrian had served two complete terms, and he announced that he was available for a third. But China, which believed the time had come for another Third World secretary general, vetoed Waldheim in the Security Council discussions. The United States, in turn, vetoed the Chinese candidate, Foreign Minister Salim Salim of Tanzania, who was perceived to be anti-American. After sixteen ballots, Waldheim and Salim withdrew, whereupon the Council agreed upon Javier Perez de Cuellar, a Peruvian diplomat with extensive experience at the United Nations. As usual, the Council's recommendation was confirmed by the General Assembly.

Waldheim's tenure, which came to a close on December 31, was not a dramatic one, to be sure. Like U Thant before him, Waldheim was cautious in his political initiatives, ever aware of the deep-seated reluctance on the part of the Security Council's permanent members, in varying degrees, to allow a reassertion of the power that Hammarskjold had accumulated, particularly during the Congo crisis. But Waldheim was energetic in providing UN peacekeeping forces when acceptable to all concerned and in offering the good offices of the secretary general in time of crisis. Again like his predecessor, Waldheim kept the United Nations together as a functioning organization, whereas a more activist secretary general might have earned the displeasure of one major power or another and thereby brought the world body to a standstill.

A major positive feature of Waldheim's terms of office was the increasing attention paid by the world body to matters that were not at a critical stage but were of universal concern and mounting urgency. These included such questions as the world environment; population control; the regulation of conduct in, on, and under the planet's international waters; and the economic relations between the poorer, lesser-developed countries and the more prosperous, developed nations. Granted, no magic solutions to these monumental problems were achieved during Waldheim's years at the helm, but beginnings were made that helped shape the course of the United Nations as it reached the mid-1980s.

6

PARTICULAR CONFLICTS AND UNIVERSAL CONCERNS

When Javier Perez de Cuellar became the organization's fifth secretary general on January 1, 1982, the seasoned Peruvian diplomat was under no illusions about the difficulties of the job ahead of him. The frustrations of his predecessors were all too well known. Moreover, Perez de Cuellar assumed his post at an inauspicious time, when the global strategic struggle between East and West had sharpened and when differences between the poverty-stricken developing world and the prosperous northern industrial countries had widened.

As to be expected, the new secretary general inherited his share of major political problems. The war between Iran and Iraq remained stalemated, and, although both sides suffered heavy casualties, they paid no heed to Security Council calls for a cessation of hostilities. Soviet troops continued to battle insurgents in Afghanistan and Vietnamese forces remained mired in Cambodia, despite repeated UN resolutions calling for the withdrawal of all "foreign" troops from both occupied countries. The

potentially explosive questions of Namibian independence and South Africa's apartheid were still far from settled. And, of course, the perennial problem of the Middle East and its seemingly insoluble Arab-Israeli conflict also awaited the attention of the new secretary general.

THE FALKLANDS

It was not long before Perez de Cuellar and the United Nations were faced with a brand-new crisis, and from an unexpected quarter. On April 1, Britain warned the Security Council of an impending Argentine invasion of the Falkland Islands, a small group of islands in the South Atlantic, some three hundred miles off the coast of Argentina. Known as the Islas Malvinas in Latin America, the sparsely populated islands had been the subject of contention between Britain and Argentina for 150 years, even though almost all the eighteen hundred sheep-tending inhabitants were of British descent and preferred to remain under British control.

The Council urged restraint, but the next day the Argentines invaded the Falklands. At that point, the Council called for "an immediate cessation of hostilities . . . (and) a withdrawal of all Argentine forces." Riding a wave of nationalist fervor, the military junta ruling in Argentina disregarded the Council's request, extended its military control and raised the Argentine flag over the islands.

The British government was taken by surprise, but it quickly dispatched a naval task force of some thirty warships to the area around the Falklands, where naval

Secretary General Javier Perez de Cuellar
addressing the General Assembly after taking
the oath of office on December 15, 1981

activity commenced on May 1. As air and naval strikes took a heavy toll on both sides, Perez de Cuellar called on Argentina and Britain to accept a cease-fire. Neither responded. After British troops landed on the islands on May 21, bitter fighting ensued; the secretary general redoubled his efforts on behalf of a cease-fire, again without success. On June 4, Britain (joined by the United States) vetoed a Security Council resolution calling for an immediate cease-fire and implementation of previous resolutions. The war ended on June 14 with the surrender of the Argentine troops, who—with the permission of the victorious British—were quickly shipped home. Once again the Union Jack flew over the Falkland Islands.

In his first major test, Perez de Cuellar had acquitted himself well. He had enhanced his personal reputation by acting with energy and impartiality. But it was clear that when two member nations have strong competing claims to territory, and when both sides have strong support among the UN membership, the role of the world body is extremely limited. An interesting point is that some Third World countries, who normally would have been expected to vote on the side of Argentina, did not do so for fear of condoning the use of force to settle territorial disputes. After the end of the Falklands war, the General Assembly repeatedly called for a resumption of negotiations between Britain and Argentina on the issue of sovereignty. Not surprisingly, the British refused, leaving the Falklands an unresolved political issue and undoubtedly an item for future UN discussion.

WAR IN LEBANON

Perez de Cuellar's first year in office was also marked by a flare-up in the Arab-Israeli conflict, this time a major Israeli invasion of Lebanon. The Israeli objective was twofold, to rid Lebanon of tens of thousands of PLO guerrillas, thereby securing Israel's northern border from attack, and to establish a Christian-dominated, solidly pro-Israel government in Lebanon. The fighting began in June 1982, when Israeli armor swept by the United Nations Interim Force in Lebanon (UNIFIL)* and quickly advanced northward against the combined opposition of PLO guerrillas, Syrian troops stationed in Lebanon, and scattered elements of the Lebanese army. In the fighting, Israeli jets, artillery, and warships took a heavy toll of civilians as well as fighting men; this was not surprising since the guerrillas, in hopes of avoiding attack, made a point of placing many of their defensive positions in heavily populated areas. The Israelis besieged the PLO-controlled sector of West Beirut from mid-June until the end of August, employing heavy bombardment despite calls by the Security Council and the General Assembly for a cease-fire and withdrawal from Lebanon.

When the PLO finally agreed to evacuate Beirut and leave the region, Israel—long at odds with the United Nations—refused to let UN observers monitor the withdrawal. As a result, it was left to four Western powers, the United States, France, Italy, and Britain, to assemble a multinational force outside UN auspices and hastily deploy it in Beirut. The force was withdrawn after the completion of the PLO evacuation in early September, only to be recalled a few weeks later to separate warring Lebanese factions. In the months that followed, Beirut and its environs were scenes of general disorder and violence, and in 1983 terrorist suicide attacks killed and wounded many American and French peacekeepers. In February 1984, the UN forces withdrew in failure.

---

*UNIFIL was dispatched to Lebanon in 1978 in the vain hope of creating a security zone north of the Israeli border; it had neither the mandate nor the arms to prevent the Israeli invasion.

Throughout much of 1983 and 1984, the fragile Lebanese government tried to pacify the country's contending factions and negotiate the withdrawal of Israeli troops. The Israelis had achieved one of their goals, the ejection of the PLO from southern Lebanon, but they had failed to create a stable, pro-Israel government in Beirut. Nevertheless, Israeli public opinion, stunned by the loss of over six hundred Israeli lives (the equivalent of forty thousand in a country the size of the United States), clamored for an end to the military adventure in Lebanon.

Until then, the United Nations, despite its many resolutions, had exercised very little influence on the course of events in Lebanon. Ever suspicious of the United Nations, the Israelis had refused to allow the world body to play a diplomatic role, instead relying on the United States to assume that position. But in 1984, stung by its experience as the major element in the Beirut peacekeeping force, the United States declined to take an active part in negotiating Israel's withdrawal. At this point, Israel and the Lebanese government had to turn to the United Nations.

In November 1984, Israeli and Lebanese military teams met at UNIFIL's headquarters at Naqura, southern Lebanon. For a time, UN officials hoped that the two sides could reach an agreement giving UNIFIL a major role in monitoring the Israeli withdrawal and providing secure northern borders for Israel. But Lebanon and Israel could not agree. In early 1985, Israel pulled out of the UN-sponsored talks and announced unilateral plans to withdraw its forces.

CENTRAL AMERICA

Historically, UN involvement in Latin American affairs had been minimal, chiefly because Western hemisphere problems often were dealt with in the Organization of

American States (OAS), the oldest and most active of the world's regional organizations. But during the first half of Perez de Cuellar's term, events in Central America— particularly the civil wars in Nicaragua and El Salvador—were frequently brought to the attention of the United Nations.

In Nicaragua, the left-wing Sandinista regime was supported and heavily armed by Soviet-bloc countries; it was opposed by armed groups called *contras,* short for *contrarevolucionarios* ("counter-revolutionaries"). The *contras,* whose ranks included rightists, democratic leftists, and disaffected Indian tribes, were in varying degrees given covert funding and technical assistance by the U.S. Central Intelligence Agency.

In El Salvador, a government once dominated by the military and by right-wing terrorists called "death squads," evolved slowly, under constant American pressure, into a freely elected, reform-minded government. With strong U.S. military and economic support, it battled left-wing insurgents backed by Nicaragua and—the United States alleged—armed by Nicaragua, Cuba, and other pro-Soviet governments.

Beginning in 1982, Nicaragua brought the question of American support for the *contras* and alleged American invasion threats before the Security Council on numerous occasions. Since the United States held the veto in the Security Council, it was clear that the Nicaraguans were using the Council to attract media attention and get their views across to the world at large. The Sandinistas also made use of the International Court of Justice, the judicial organ of the United Nations. In April 1984, it was asked to rule on the legality of U.S. involvement in the mining of Nicaraguan ports. The United States informed the United Nations that it would not accept the Court's jurisdiction in this case, but in May the Court handed the United States a setback by refusing to remove the case from its docket.

In the early 1980s, El Salvador was the target of consistent attack at the United Nations by Communist bloc and left-wing Third World countries for alleged complicity with the right-wing terrorists. But after the election of Jose Napoleon Duarte, a moderate Christian Democrat, as president of El Salvador in May of 1984, the critical rhetoric subsided. Indeed, the widely respected Duarte made a dramatic appearance before the General Assembly in October of 1984, when he stunned the delegates by agreeing to meet with insurgent leaders at La Palma, El Salvador, with no armed forces of either side in attendance. The meeting actually took place a few weeks later, and though it was civil in tone neither side altered its position. Duarte insisted that the rebels lay down their arms and participate in the country's developing democratic process. The insurgents argued that they would have to be given a substantial role in the government before they would give up their armed struggle and take part in elections.

For all the rhetoric expended at the United Nations on the subject of Central America, the world body remained on the periphery of diplomatic activity concerning the region. The United States, as chief supporter of El Salvador and adversary of the Sandinista government of Nicaragua, played a key role, but perhaps the most potentially creative diplomatic contribution came from the so-called Contadora Group. This group of countries, Mexico, Colombia, Panama, and Venezuela, was named after the tiny Panamanian island where they first met to ponder the problem of creating a stable, democratic Central America.

During the course of 1984, the Contadora countries produced a draft of a treaty for circulation among the Central American countries. Although supposedly a secret document for use as the basis for further discussion and amendment, the draft reportedly called for noninterference in the affairs of other states, limitations on arms, the withdrawal of all foreign troops and advisers, and a commitment to "democratic pluralism." Nicaragua indicated that it might accept such a treaty, but the United States and some of its allies in the region, Costa Rica, Honduras, and El Salvador, were arguing for amendments that would allow for verification procedures to make certain that all sides actually lived up to the provisions.

UNIVERSAL CONCERNS

The international issues discussed in this chapter and previous ones involved conflicts—often dangerous and bloody—between member countries of the United Nations, or between groups within those states. But other kinds of questions, those of concern to mankind at large, have come to the forefront at the world body in recent years. These include questions of human rights and race segregation; the status of women, children, and the aged; and also environmental, economic, and social issues that literally affect the lives of billions of people around the world. We will examine some of them in the pages that follow:

• *The Environment.* The United Nations Environment Program (UNEP) was established in 1972 to protect and improve natural surroundings. But despite enormous global environmental problems, some of them urgently in need of remedy, the program has suffered from an astonishing amount of indifference on the part of UN members of every political hue.

One of the gravest problems facing the world today is "desertification"—the transformation of formerly cultivatable land into sterile desert waste. One estimate is that areas throughout the world equivalent to the total square miles of China have been turned into desert, in part because of shifting weather patterns but mainly

*A young girl runs through newly planted cedar trees
in Senegal. Such plantings prevent the desert
from spreading, but UN members must develop and
fund a more comprehensive program if the
devastating problem of desertification is to be conquered.*

because of human ignorance and ineptitude. This growing desertification has affected the lives of some 680 million people in sixty-three countries.

Africa has been hardest hit. Desertification and years of drought have had a devastating effect on food production in twenty-four African countries. Ethiopia, Mauritania, and Mozambique have been the most seriously affected, but emergency food aid has been rushed to other countries as well, in an effort to prevent the starvation of hundreds of thousands, perhaps millions, of people.

For years UNEP pleaded with the members of the United Nations for the funding and technical assistance needed to cope with this truly enormous world problem. It has also lobbied hard for programs to protect regional seas and marine life, to guard against soil erosion, and to monitor the distribution of toxic chemicals. In 1985 it will convene a conference on the "protection of the ozone layer." UNEP will seek the cooperation of all UN members in finding ways to protect "man and the environment from changes in the ozone layer caused by worldwide emissions of chlorofluorocarbons (CFCs) and other compounds." Unless the ozone layer is protected, UNEP scientists believe, there could be an increase in the amount of ultraviolet light reaching the earth and consequently a higher incidence of skin cancer.

Most governments recognize the gravity of these global concerns and agree in principle with programs UNEP has designed to address them. But all too clearly the governments of the world lack real commitment to environmental problems and have refused to give UNEP adequate funding. "The governments of the world have obtained the UN agency they deserve," commented a report by a group of nongovernmental environmentalists. "They have contributed [in 1982] only $30 million to the Environment Fund, less than is spent in half-an-hour on armaments."

• *Food and Agriculture.* Since the beginning of the United Nations, its Food and Agriculture Organization (FAO) has tried to help countries improve agriculture, increase food production, and alleviate hunger. But in the past decade, as food scarcity and starvation afflicted millions, UN members established two additional agencies: the World Food Council (WFC) and the International Fund for Agricultural Development (IFAD).

The problem of hunger is an everyday one in many parts of the world. Although Asians have made gains in food production, the region still had the largest number of chronically undernourished people in 1984. In Latin America, fifty million people suffered from malnutrition, about 15 percent of the total population. The food problem in Africa was even worse—more critical than anywhere in the world. African agriculture had been stifled by drought, desertification, animal disease, and heavy crop infestation; food production simply was not keeping pace with the rapid population growth. Africa's food deficit in 1984 alone was three million tons, twice as large as in 1983, when hundreds of thousands died of starvation.

In large part the desperate food shortages faced by more than 150 million sub-Saharan Africans in the mid-1980s was due to policies pursued by governments of the region. Some discouraged food production by favoring artifically low consumer prices in the cities—where high food prices might cause political discontent—at the expense of price incentives for farmers. Others encouraged the production of goods for export to earn foreign exchange to finance imports; food production for domestic consumption was neglected. Many governments bought expensive military equipment and spent little on the roads and railways that might have brought food to the hungry. In Ethiopia, for example, many parts of the south enjoyed food surpluses even as people starved in the north.

Under difficult circumstance, UN agencies did what they could to deal with Africa's food crisis.* In 1984, as much as 40 percent of FAO's regular budget was allocated exclusively for the benefit of the sub-Saharan countries. Moreover, the FAO repeatedly tried to secure additional pledges of food aid from donor countries and urged them to speed delivery time. On a longer-term basis, the World Food Council stepped up efforts to help food-poor countries develop "national food strategies" to pinpoint food needs, plan solutions, and prepare for shortages in the years ahead. Similarly, the International Fund for Agricultural Development pushed ahead with projects for improving irrigation, land settlement, fisheries, and credit institutions for small farmers and landless workers.

Not everyone applauded the efforts of the UN agencies. Some private international relief organizations complained that overlapping among the various UN agencies made it difficult to coordinate with them and that bickering among the UN agencies wasted valuable time in getting food to the needy. Even more important, many major donor nations chose to ignore the United Nations and make their contributions on a direct, country-to-country basis. The United States, the chief donor of food assistance, chose to funnel only 8 percent of its aid through multilateral organizations (including the United Nations). The United States was not alone in this policy. Countries contributing aid usually like the recipients to know where it is coming from.

• *Population.* The International Conference on Population was held in Mexico City under UN auspices in August 1984 to review world population trends and

*It should be remembered that many private relief organizations and governmental agencies also made major, critically important contributions.

make recommendations for action by UN organs and member states. The conference took place at a time when most of the delegates did not regard the world population outlook as encouraging. There were approximately 4.8 billion people in the world, a number that was expected to double by the end of the next (twenty-first) century. More people were born in 1983 than in any other year in history, even though population growth rates were beginning to decline. Demographic experts estimated that the rate of population growth would continue to fall slowly, so that world population would level off at about ten billion around the year 2100.

On the surface, that overall global trend seemed encouraging. But as many delegates pointed out, the overall world population rate masked the enormous difference between rates in the developed countries, where populations are expanding by less than 1 percent, and the developing countries, where they are growing at annual rates of from 2 to 4 percent. At these rates, the populations of the developed world will double every seventy years, while the populations of the developing world will increase eightfold during the same period. Between 1984 and the year 2025, it was estimated, Africa's population will quadruple; the populations of Latin America and Asia will double. Unless checked, this population explosion in the developing world is expected to cause chronic food shortages, political instability, and an ever greater chasm between the standards of living of the richer and poorer nations.

Some Third World countries nearly derailed the Mexico City conference by introducing issues more concerned with politics—such as Israeli settlement policy on the occupied West Bank—than with population. And there was sharp contention between countries like the United States, which opposed the practice of abortion in state family-planning programs or the use of government coercion to achieve family planning, and Third World countries which supported strong measures if necessary to check population growth. The United States delegation also argued that the adoption of free market economies would create the kind of fundamental development that would reduce population growth without strong governmental programs. This view was rejected by most delegations, and by A. W. Clausen, an American who heads the World Bank. "In some countries development may not be possible," he warned, "unless lower [population] growth rates are achieved."

Despite opposition to the American position, delegates were aware that the United States contributes about $240 million annually for population-control programs worldwide, about half of all assistance available. As a result, the conference's final declaration avoided language that might be construed by the United States as critical and stressed the consensus that family planning and economic growth were the two keys to population control and the maintenance of living standards.

The United Nations Fund for Population Activities, which played a major role in organizing the International Conference on Population, is the major UN agency dealing with population. When it began in 1969, UNFPA stressed the collection of basic data on population; in recent years it has shifted its emphasis to helping countries with population problems devise educational and family planning programs.

• *Law of the Sea.* Ever since 1958, the United Nations has been attempting to formulate a Law of the Sea covering almost all human uses of the seas—navigation, overflight, resource exploration and exploitation, conservation and pollution, fishing, and shipping. After years of analysis, argument, and give-and-take in UN conferences and committees, in which all members took part, a treaty—or Convention, as it is called—was produced in 1982. Its 321 articles and 9 annexes, which constitute a guide for behavior by nations in the world's oceans, amount to a potentially enormous achievement in international law. Some key provisions:

(a) Coastal states would exercise sovereignty over their *territorial waters* to a distance of twelve miles, but foreign vessels would be permitted "innocent passage" through such waters for purposes of peaceful navigation.

(b) Ships and aircraft of all nations would be permitted "transit passage" through *straits used for international navigation*, as long as they proceeded without delay and without threatening bordering states.

(c) Coastal states would have sovereign rights to natural resources, certain economic research activities, and marine science research in a 200-mile *exclusive economic zone*. All other states would have freedom of navigation and overflight in the zone, as well as freedom to lay submarine pipelines and cables.

(d) Coastal states would have sovereign rights over the *continental shelf* extending from its shores for the purposes of exploring and exploiting it for oil and other resources.

(e) Landlocked states would have the right of access to and from the seas, and coastal states bordering on the landlocked countries would be expected to cooperate.

(f) A "parallel system" would be established for exploring and exploiting the *international seabed area*; all activities in this area would be under the control of the International Seabed Authority, to be established by the Convention; the Authority would be authorized to conduct its own seabed mining operations through an operating arm called the Enterprise; the Authority also would be able to contract with private or governmental organizations in any part of the world and to give them mining

(102)

rights in parts of the international seabed area, so that they would operate in parallel with the Authority.

(g) States would be bound to promote the *development and transfer of marine technology* on "fair and reasonable terms and conditions."

(h) States would be obliged to settle by peaceful means their *disputes* over the interpretation and application of the Convention; they would have to submit most types of disputes to a compulsory procedure entailing decisions binding on all parties.

The text of the new Convention was approved at UN headquarters in New York on April 30, 1982, by a vote of 130 in favor to 4 against, with 17 abstentions. The document was signed by 117 states at a formal ceremony at Montego Bay, Jamaica, in December, and it will enter into force twelve months after it is ratified by 60 states.

As of the mid-1980s, however, the future of the Convention is by no means clear. During the Reagan administration, the United States refused to sign it. The United States supported most of the treaty but had deep reservations about the establishment of a Seabed Authority with the power to determine who should be permitted to mine the seabed in international waters and to conduct mining operations itself. It also disagreed with the provision on the development and transfer of marine technology, since it might mean that American developers of marine technology would be compelled to turn it over to private competitors or foreign states. This American coolness toward these points in the Convention is shared by other developed countries with the technology and know-how to begin seabed mining without delay and without the approval of an international authority.

Most members of the United Nations, including many pro-American countries, are distressed by the U.S.

refusal to sign the Convention. Given the uncertainty, there has been no great rush to ratify it. In mid-1984, two years after the signing at Jamaica, only ten member states had ratified the Convention.

• *New Economic Order.* Since the mid-1970s, the New International Economic Order (NIEO), with its call for a thorough transformation of the world's economy, has been the most prominent economic issue before the United Nations. It has also been an ill-defined and controversial issue, pitting the developing countries of the South against the developed industrial countries of the North.

In 1974, at a special session of the General Assembly on "raw materials and development," the Third World majority pushed through a "Declaration on the Establishment of a New Economic Order" and an "Action Program" to carry it out. In the declaration, member states solemnly proclaimed their determination to work urgently for "the establishment of a new international economic order" which would "correct inequalities and redress existing injustices, make it possible to eliminate the widening gap between the developed and developing countries, and insure steadily accelerating economic and social development in peace and justice for the present and future generations."

The program of action envisioned by the backers of the new order—and particularly the more militant members of the Third World and their Soviet-bloc allies— amounted to nothing less than a total overhaul of the international economy. The major overall objective was the transformation of the economies of developing countries. To this end, the action program demanded greater access to Western markets for Third World goods, particularly its manufactures; higher and more stable prices for their raw materials; freer access to Western technology; curbs on the operations of multinational corporations, particularly in the extractive industries (mining and oil drilling); lower and inflation-proof prices for their imports from the developed world; and finally, a far greater share in the management of the world economy in such institutions as the World Bank and the International Monetary Fund.

At the time these proposals were made, the Third World may have thought they were attainable. After all, in the mid-1970s, the Organization of Petroleum Exporting Countries (OPEC) was demonstrating that its cartel could raise world oil prices and play havoc with the economies of the developed countries. However, in several conferences between countries of the North and those of the South, the large issues raised by the declaration and action program were discussed and rediscussed, with little practical result. Clearly, the developed countries had no intention of submitting to such a radical restructuring of the world economy, and by the early 1980s many Third World leaders realized that they had set their sights too high. Attainable goals, with immediate economic impact, were needed.

There were a number of reasons for this apparent Third World retreat. For one thing, OPEC fell into disarray and decline as an influence on the world economy, depriving the Third World of a strong ally in its dealings with the developed countries. In addition, a worldwide recession confronted many Third World countries with falling exports, smaller hard-currency income, and a consequent inability to pay their enormous foreign debts. In such a situation, many Third World countries became far more interested in practical matters such as increased foreign investment, easier terms for debt repayment, and direct economic assistance from the developed countries. At a meeting of the Third World countries in Buenos Aires in 1984, Farouk Sobhan of Bangladesh summed up the general view when he stated that "we cannot change institutions overnight, we have to do this gradually with a sense of purpose and pragmatism."

This certainly does not mean that the Third World

countries at the United Nations have given up hopes of a major, long-term restructuring of the international economy. But it does mean that changes will come in a gradual, step-by-step fashion, so that they will not produce severe jolts to developed countries or overnight economic utopia for the Third World.

• *The Information Question—and UNESCO.* Perhaps no question debated at the United Nations in recent years has aroused so much Western hostility as attempts by the Soviet bloc and some Third World countries to establish what they call a "New World Information and Communication Order (NWICO)." The main forum for debate on this issue has been the United Nations Educational, Scientific and Cultural Organization (UNESCO), whose leadership has come under Western fire, particularly from the United States, for its espousal of NWICO and for a number of other reasons.

UNESCO was conceived in the spirit of idealism that prompted the founding of the United Nations itself. With the educational systems of many nations crippled by World War II and with the war itself demonstrating the importance of science, it seemed logical to establish an organization dedicated to educational and cultural exchanges as well as the furtherance of scientific inquiry. In many ways, UNESCO has lived up to its expectations. It provided for the training of teachers in many poor countries, helped to build schools, and worked to eradicate illiteracy. It helped to bring television into remote areas of the world; it even became involved in campaigns to save ancient monuments.

So far, so good. But since the mid-1970s, when the full impact of the Third World majority began to be felt, the organization has taken on an increasingly political tinge. As in other UN agencies, Israel comes under consistent attack. But the heart of the matter is the tendency of UNESCO's administrative leadership to embrace the

(106)

views of the Soviet bloc and the Third World on such irrelevant topics as the international economy and disarmament. These questions, say the United States and others, should not be taking up the time of an organization supposedly dedicated to the advancement of education, culture, and science.

A major area of contention has been the attempt by the Third World and the Soviet Union—with the support of UNESCO's director general, Amadou-Mahtar M'Bow of Senegal—to promote a so-called "new world information order." One objective is to end the dominance of the Western press, which is portrayed as a threat to the "cultural identity" of the Third World and its citizens, who are "passive receivers" of news disseminated by Western media. As a matter of fact, many Western observers agree that the Third World should be helped with technology, expertise, and access to satellites to improve their own communications systems and decrease their dependence on Western news sources.

Other aspects of the proposed "new world information order," however, are totally objectionable to Western governments and the Western media. The dispute involves a basic difference of philosophy on the role of the media in society. The Soviets and many Third World countries contend that the press is an instrument of society that should be used to further the objectives of the state and that governments should control information for the good of society at large. The Western view is that a free press, inquiring about and critical of government and all aspects of life, is necessary to an informed citizenry, which can then make informed policy decisions. And the Western press, of course, reflects diverse opinions rather than those of governments.

In more concrete terms, supporters of the new world information order would like UNESCO to pass a series of resolutions that would encourage Third World governments to impose restrictions on the Western press and endorse the notion that governments have the right to control information for their own ends. They would like UNESCO to draw up an international "code of conduct" for journalists, enshrining Third World ideas of how the press should behave, and also issue UNESCO identification cards to journalists, which could be revoked if journalists were found to be in breach of the code of conduct. This, contend Western media spokesmen, would amount to a licensing system by UNESCO, which could withhold ID cards from those journalists that particular governments found objectionable.

In addition to the information question and UNESCO's leftward tilt, the Reagan administration and other Western governments have charged that the organization is a hotbed of mismanagement, nepotism, and overspending. In 1983, the United States, which provides 25 percent of UNESCO's budget, warned the United Nations that it would drop its membership in UNESCO unless major changes were made; other Western countries have warned of possible similar action. At the end of 1984, the United States did withdraw, and it was far from clear what the future held in store for the new world information order—or for UNESCO.

A PATIENT HORSE

For Secretary General Perez de Cuellar, the particular conflicts and universal concerns touched on here were only part of the discouraging picture at the United Nations. As he well knew, the organization is more than ever divided by ideology, nationalism, economic disparity, and cultural difference, and that situation is unlikely to change for some time to come. In his third annual report to the General Assembly, delivered in September 1984, the secretary general was, as usual, somewhat pessimistic. A sensitive man, he is well aware of the criticism of the organization, and in his report he once again defended the institution but complained of its neglect or misuse by member countries.

As Perez de Cuellar pointed out, the conflict between the superpowers continued to incapacitate the Security Council, once thought of as the primary guarantor of peace and security in the world. "The majestic vision" of the United Nations, he said, has been "clouded by the differences of the major powers." The inability of the Council to act has led to a sidestepping of the United Nations in favor of force or unilateral action, or "a retreat from internationalism."

Without pointing fingers, the secretary general also directed some critical words at the Third World and its conduct as the overwhelming majority in the General Assembly. He took note of the repetitious agenda items, the superfluity of resolutions, and the indifference with which the world reacts to them. "The non-implementation of resolutions, as well as their proliferation," observed the secretary general, "has tended to downgrade the seriousness with which governments and the public take the decisions of the United Nations."

On the subject of the UN machinery and its misuse by member countries, Perez de Cuellar added: "The United Nations is a patient horse, but it should not be ridden to a standstill without thought of the consequences."

WHERE IS
THE UN HEADED?

As the United Nations approached its fortieth birthday, Americans viewed the world organization with decidedly mixed feelings. Many of them also wondered whether it might not be time for reform of the rickety diplomatic edifice erected in San Francisco in 1945.

AMERICAN MOOD

In the mid-1980s, many Americans in high places seemed eager to take off their kid gloves in dealing with the United Nations. As mentioned earlier, the Reagan administration actually withdrew from UNESCO in protest over what it considered to be biased proceedings and bungling management. Washington was also watching other UN agencies closely in case similar action was warranted.

At UN headquarters in New York, President Reagan's ambassador to the United Nations, Jean Kirkpatrick, also caused some nervous fluttering by publicly stating that it was administration policy to take a country's voting record into account when it came time to assess how much aid to give it. The U.S. Congress went even further. In November 1983, it passed legislation that *required* the cutting off of *all* aid to countries that consistently oppose American policy at the United Nations.

Other signs of American impatience with the goings-on at the United Nations were not hard to find. The influential, conservative, Washington-based Heritage Foundation issued a steady stream of attacks, contending that the United Nations had turned into an anti-American club dominated by the Soviet bloc, European leftists, and radical countries in the Third World. Some Heritage Foundation literature threw up its hands and called for a U.S. withdrawal from the United Nations. Even the *New York Times Magazine*, not known for its sensationalism, published a long critical article on the United Nations with the inflammatory headline: "The U.N. Versus the U.S." Perhaps the most colorful expression of this mood of confrontation came from Charles Lichenstein, one of Ambassador Kirkpatrick's top deputies. When various UN delegates, irritated by one U.S. position or another, suggested that UN headquarters be moved out of the United States, Lichenstein stunned a Security Council session by stating: "We will put no impediment in your way. The members of the United States Mission to the United Nations will be down at dockside waving you a fond farewell as you sail into the sunset." An undiplomatic remark, perhaps, but it did squelch loose talk about moving UN headquarters.

The American public, too, had lost some confidence in the United Nations. Polls taken in the early 1980s showed a declining number of Americans who thought the United Nations was "doing a good job." A Roper poll in June 1983 broke down American opinion as follows:

Poor Job—42 percent
Good Job—35 percent
Other—23 percent

At the same time, the Roper poll and others showed that the American people had by no means lost faith in the United Nations. Asked by the Roper poll whether the United States should remain in the United Nations, the response was:

Remain—89 percent
Withdraw—5 percent
Other—6 percent

Interestingly, the same Roper poll also showed that a solid majority of Americans would like to see the United Nations have more power, not less, in the following areas: reducing the danger of superpower confrontation, supporting human rights, conserving natural resources, and helping poor countries develop. It is noteworthy that the American public, according to the polls, is critical of the performance of the United Nations and yet wants the United States to continue its membership. It may be even more noteworthy that a sizable majority of Americans actually would like to see the United Nations have more power to act in certain important areas of universal concern. The question was not posed, but it seems fair to deduce that the American public would also support a degree of change in the way the United Nations now operates.

REFORM POSSIBILITIES

The founders of the United Nations did not foresee that a global strategic struggle between nuclear superpowers would all but paralyze the Security Council, which they hoped would be the major force in keeping world peace. Nor could they guess that the historic process of decolonization would swell UN membership to the unwieldy

(112)

numbers it achieved in the mid-1980s. In 1984, there were 159 members, ranging from China with a quarter of the world's more than four billion people to micro-dot countries like the Seychelles with seventy thousand. Clearly, a fresh look at the United Nations was in order.

Ideas for reforming the United Nations usually start in the most obvious places: the Security Council and the General Assembly. The proposals normally center on the veto power in the Council and the voting system in the Assembly.

Amending the UN Charter to do away with the veto is not possible at this time. None of the five permanent members of the Security Council (the United States, the Soviet Union, Britain, France, and China) would stand for it. Egypt has presented a proposal that would have the Big Five agree "informally" to exempt a large number of decisions from the veto. The list of exemptions would include Council resolutions to send fact-finders or observers with host-country consent; resolutions authorizing the secretary general to pursue mediation efforts; resolutions calling for cease-fires, separation of forces, or withdrawal behind national borders once hostilities have broken out. Other proposals would also exempt resolutions concerning disputes to which the veto-bearing permanent Council members are a party.

Does this kind of "gentleman's agreement" to limit the use of the veto have a chance of succeeding? "Anything can happen," comments a top Secretariat official, "but don't bet your farm on it. The Big Five are in no mood to permit the lessening of their power in any way." That seemed to be the general consensus in the UN community in the mid-1980s.

Over the years, many proposals have been made to reform the manifestly absurd voting situation in the General Assembly. One vote for each sovereign country has a nice ring to it, but in practice it has produced diplomatic bedlam: endless speechmaking, pointless resolutions, and a bored, indifferent public. One reform proposal would offer the many mini-states an "associate state" status, which would enable them to enjoy the economic benefits of UN membership without the financial burdens or voting privileges of full membership. In addition, there are many proposals for "weighted voting." This would entail votes reflecting the members' population, economic strength, or financial contribution to the organization, or a formula taking into account all these factors.

The problem with all this is that it would require changes in the Charter, and that is unlikely to happen. The individual members, no matter how small or how poor, are jealous of their rights as sovereign countries. Many of the newly independent mini-states take keen satisfaction in being treated with the same outward respect as the United States, the Soviet Union, China, and Europe's ancient states.

As far as the Security Council and the General Assembly are concerned, then, it looks as if the future will be "more of the same." But there are areas in which real change is possible, and all of them are extremely important. None would require Charter revision and none concern the political organs of the world body. Within the next decade, the following developments are probable:

- The creation of a UN-supervised international system for the storage and distribution of food reserves in times of famine.
- A modification of the world's trading system to make it more responsive to the needs of the Third World; for instance, the establishment by the World Bank of a large fund to help moderate the commodity price fluctuations that are so disastrous to undiversified agricultural economies.

- The strengthening of the United Nations Environment Program (UNEP) to reflect a growing world consciousness about the need to prevent desertification, pollution, and other environmental hazards.
- The signing and ratification of the Law of the Sea Convention by the necessary sixty countries; the International Seabed authority commences to regulate mining in the international seabed.

These changes may not be what people have in mind when they think of reforming the United Nations. These changes will not be headline-makers. But they will make the United Nations stronger and will have a significant impact on the world we live in by the year 2000.

A GREAT DEBATE?

As for the political institutions of the United Nations, the Security Council and the General Assembly, the world will simply have to make do with what it has. It would take an incredible crisis, perhaps even a brush with nuclear catastrophe to bring about significant changes in either the Council or the Assembly. In the meantime, these UN political organs may not be as sterile as they sometimes seem. Writes Donald J. Puchala, professor of government at the University of South Carolina:

> *But the UN's current lack of decisiveness and impact may also tell something about its present historical context. A long era—the age of the great European empires—has recently ended, and the United Nations contributed to its passing. Now, a new phase in world history is beginning, and the kinds of values and institutions that will characterize and shape it are in dispute.*

(115)

Therefore, what some call "stagnation" within the United Nations might be more revealingly identified as a great debate. What we are witnessing worldwide, and what is greatly amplified within the organization where interactions are structured and focused, is the profound and global confrontation of peoples' ideas and ideals. . . . The great debate is about the foundations of the 21st century world order; it is all-encompassing.

Professor Puchala makes a good case for the United Nations as the forum for a great debate that will chart our way into the next century. That may well be. For the time being, the United Nations also provides the nations of the world with an invaluable piece of machinery; it is up to them to use it properly. And for all its failings, the United Nations is a significant reality of our time. Few people anywhere would be foolish enough to wish an end to it. Without the United Nations, as Secretary General Perez de Cuellar correctly states, "the world would certainly be a much more dangerous and disorderly place."

FOR FURTHER
READING

Not surprisingly, the best books about the United
Nations are those written by people with firsthand experience at top levels of the organization. Among these are
In the Cause of Peace by Trygve Lie (New York: Macmil-
lan, 1954), a revealing account of his eventful tenure in
office by the world body's first secretary general. A far
different kind of book is *Building the Future Order* by
Kurt Waldheim (New York: Free Press, 1980), a
thoughtful assessment of the United Nations and its
future by its fourth secretary general.

An excellent book on a vital period in UN history—
and on the most remarkable leader the organization has
had—is *Hammarskjold* by Brian Urquhart (New York:
Alfred A. Knopf, 1972). A high-level official in the Secretariat since its earliest days and a close associate of the
second secretary general, Urquhart presents a vivid picture of the accomplishments and failures of the Hammarskjold years.

Two books by Conor Cruise O'Brien, a top UN official during the Congo crisis of the early 1960s, are of particular interest. In *To Katanga and Back* (New York: Simon and Schuster, 1963), the Irish diplomat and literary figure gives a personal account of how the United Nations coped with an extremely difficult situation in a volatile part of Africa. In *The United Nations: Sacred Drama* (New York: Simon and Schuster, 1968), O'Brien takes an original view of the United Nations as a stage-setting for the continuous dramatization of current world history.

In *The Play Within the Play* (New York: Alfred A. Knopf, 1966), Hernane Tavares de Sá, a onetime UN undersecretary for public information, presents a fascinating description of how the United Nations operates behind the scenes and on a personal level. Another book by a former Secretariat official is *Defeat of an Ideal* by Shirley Hazzard (Boston: Little, Brown & Co., 1973), an insider's critical examination of how the United Nations operated during the tenures of Secretary Generals Lie, Hammarskjold, and U Thant. Journalist and social critic William F. Buckley, who served as a member of the U.S. delegation to the twenty-eighth session of the General Assembly in 1973, published his tart observations on that experience in *United Nations Journal* (New York: Anchor Books, 1977).

There are many books by scholars and academics about the United Nations. *The United Nations as a Political Institution* by H. G. Nicholas (New York: Oxford University Press, 1975), is a sensible examination of the origins of the United Nations and the functions of its various branches. *Soldiers Without Enemies* by Larry Fabian (Washington: Brookings Institution, 1971) analyses the world organization's successes and failures in the realm of peacekeeping. A variety of scholarly views on the United Nations and the U.S. role in the organization is collected in *The U.S., the UN, and the Manage-*

ment of Global Change, ed. Toby Trister Gati (New York: New York University Press, 1983).

The United Nations itself has published a number of useful books and booklets. Among them are such handy reference works as *Basic Facts About the United Nations, Everyman's United Nations,* and *Your United Nations.* Also available are publications on specialized subjects such as *The United Nations and Decolonization, The United Nations and Outer Space,* and *The United Nations and Human Rights.* For a complete list of UN publications in print and on sale, write to United Nations Publications, Room A-3315, United Nations, New York, New York 10017, U.S.A.

Another rich source of information on the United Nations is the United Nations Association of the United States. For a complete list of available books, pamphlets, and educational materials, write to Publications Coordinator, UNA-USA, 300 East 42nd Street, New York, New York 10017. UNA-USA also publishes *The Inter Dependent,* a bimonthly periodical containing news and analysis of current topics of concern to the United Nations.

Students who wish to keep abreast of UN affairs should also consult appropriate newspapers, news magazines, and scholarly journals. For background and history, the *Encyclopedia Britannica* and the *Encyclopedia Americana* are often quite useful.

INDEX